Cross-platform Localization for Native Mobile Apps with Xamarin

Christopher Miller

Apress®

Cross-platform Localization for Native Mobile Apps with Xamarin

Christopher Miller
Slingerlands, New York
USA

ISBN-13 (pbk): 978-1-4842-2465-6   ISBN-13 (electronic): 978-1-4842-2466-3
DOI 10.1007/978-1-4842-2466-3

Library of Congress Control Number: 2016961811

Managing Director: Welmoed Spahr
Lead Editor: Todd Green
Development Editor: Laura Berendson
Technical Reviewer: Craig Dunn and Cameron Lerum
Editorial Board: Steve Anglin, Pramila Balan, Laura Berendson, Aaron Black, Louise Corrigan, Jonathan Gennick, Todd Green, Robert Hutchinson, Celestin Suresh John, Nikhil Karkal, James Markham, Susan McDermott, Matthew Moodie, Natalie Pao, Gwenan Spearing
Coordinating Editor: Jill Balzano
Copy Editor: Nancy Sixsmith
Compositor: SPi Global
Indexer: SPi Global
Artist: SPi Global

Distributed to the book trade worldwide by Springer Science+Business Media New York, 233 Spring Street, 6th Floor, New York, NY 10013. Phone 1-800-SPRINGER, fax (201) 348-4505, e-mail orders-ny@springer-sbm.com, or visit www.springer.com. Apress Media, LLC is a California LLC and the sole member (owner) is Springer Science + Business Media Finance Inc (SSBM Finance Inc). SSBM Finance Inc is a **Delaware** corporation.

For information on translations, please e-mail rights@apress.com, or visit www.apress.com.

Apress and friends of ED books may be purchased in bulk for academic, corporate, or promotional use. eBook versions and licenses are also available for most titles. For more information, reference our Special Bulk Sales–eBook Licensing web page at www.apress.com/bulk-sales.

Any source code or other supplementary materials referenced by the author in this text are available to readers at www.apress.com. For detailed information about how to locate your book's source code, go to www.apress.com/source-code/. Readers can also access source code at SpringerLink in the Supplementary Material section for each chapter.

Printed on acid-free paper

I dedicate this book to my wife, Anne, and to my daughters, Kathryn and Laura.
They are what made this book possible.

Contents at a Glance

Contents

About the Author

Chris Miller is a software architect for Tyler Technologies. He is a Microsoft MVP for .NET and is active in the local developer community. Chris is a Microsoft Certified Professional and a Xamarin Certified Mobile Developer. His experience covers back-end development work in ASP.NET and SQL Server, and front-end work with Xamarin and other Microsoft technologies. Chris maintains a blog at www.rajapet.com and can be followed on Twitter as @anotherlab. Chris lives in upstate New York with his wife and daughters.

Acknowledgments

I would like to thank the following people for the language translations that were provided for the "Island Menu" sample application:

My coworker, David Krings, for the German text

From SmartCAT.ai: Maximiliano Diaz for the Spanish text and Maxim Morkovkin for the Chinese (Simplified) text

And a thank you to Vladimir "Vova" Zakharov of SmartCAT for arranging the translations. SmartCAT provides an online service that matches freelance translators with clients.

CHAPTER 1

What Is Localization?

Before anything else, preparation is the key to success.

—Alexander Graham Bell

What Is Localization, and Why Should You Pay for it?

This book is written for the native app developer who wants to support multiple languages and cultures with a shared code base.

I'll cover definitions in the following sections, but for now just know that *localization* is part of the process that lets you put your app out in as many markets as you can. The app stores are global, and your app should be, too. This chapter focuses on native mobile app development and how to get from one language to multiple languages. You will learn about Android, iOS, and Windows 10 by using Microsoft Visual Studio and its Xamarin product.

Let's start with some of the definitions. The common terms are *localization* and *internationalization*. They are distinct but related, and you need to handle both to make your app a global app.

Internationalization

Internationalization is the process of adapting your application to work with multiple regions and countries with the same code base. One example of internationalization is the handling of number formatting. The character that defines the decimal place is referred to as a *decimal mark*. The United States and Great Britain use a period as the decimal mark: 45.36. In other countries, such as France and Germany, a comma is used to indicate the decimal place: 45,36.

Some countries use multiple formats. In Canada, a period is used as the decimal mark when the language used is English. When French is used, the comma is the decimal mark.

Also associated with the decimal mark is the character used as the thousands separator for digit grouping. When the decimal mark changes with the language selection, the thousands separator changes along with it. When a period is used as a decimal mark, the thousands separator is the comma. When a comma is the decimal mark, a space is used as the thousands separator.

Although the period and the comma are the most common versions of the decimal mark, other formats are also in use. In Arabic, the decimal mark is a Unicode character called the Arabic decimal separator ".", and the thousands separator looks like this: " ، "

Note For more information about the decimal mark, please see the Wikipedia article posted at `https://en.wikipedia.org/wiki/Decimal_mark`.

Electronic supplementary material The online version of this chapter (doi:DOI 10.1007/978-1-4842-2466-3_1) contains supplementary material, which is available to authorized users.

Another example of internationalization is the way dates are displayed numerically. Does the month come first, or does the day come first? That depends entirely on the culture.

When you see the date shown as 1/11/2016, it represents January 11th, 2016 to an American. A user in Great Britain reads it as November 1st, 2016. It's important to be able to display data in the format that the user is expecting.

When writing your application to support internationalization, you will use the frameworks or libraries that are part of your development system to correctly pick the correct decimal mark character. This character is based on the user's language and country settings, which are provided to your app by the OS.

Localization

Localization is the process of adapting your application from one language to multiple languages. You separate the text strings (and other resources such as images, video, and audio, if present) from your application so they can be translated into the languages that you plan to support. When the app runs, the resources for the end user are displayed that match the user's language and country preferences.

You may see internationalization abbreviated as *i18n*, where the *18* stands for the number of letters between the starting *i* and the ending *n* in *internationalization*. Similarly, you can see localization abbreviated as *l10n*. The technical term for this type of abbreviation is a *numeronym*. Other examples of numeronyms include *K9* for *canine* and *W3C* for *World Wide Web Consortium*.

Why Do You Want to Do This?

The big reason why you should internationalize is this: the more languages and cultures that you can support, the larger the audience will be for your application. The larger the audience, the more money you can earn from your application. That money can come from sales of the application, increased ad revenue, or indirectly as part of a larger application.

Global Marketplace

The market for mobile applications is a global one. Each of the app stores provides support for multiple regions. The more languages and cultures that you can support, the greater the audience will be for your app.

Let's Talk About the Numbers

The two largest app stores, the Apple iOS App Store and Google Play, provide detailed statistics on app downloads and revenues.

▓ **Note**   China has multiple app stores for Android apps. Being able to support multiple apps stores is vital if the Chinese market is important to you. The Google Play store currently allows only free apps in China; paid apps are barred.

Companies such as App Annie generate reports that provide breakdowns of app downloads and sales across the worldwide markets. Figure 1-1 shows recent trends for the top three countries for iOS App Store revenue.

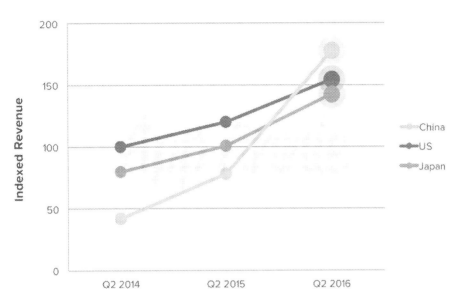

Top 3 Countries by Quarterly iOS App Store Games Revenue

Figure 1-1. *Top three countries by quarterly iOS App Store games revenue Source: App Annie Index, Market Q3, 2016.*

Until this year, the leader in game revenue for iOS was the United States, but China beat the United States in early 2016. So if you are writing a game for iOS, you don't want to ignore the Chinese market.

For worldwide app downloads, if you look at the numbers gathered by App Annie, it becomes readily apparent that the global app market is much large than the US market (see Figure 1-2).

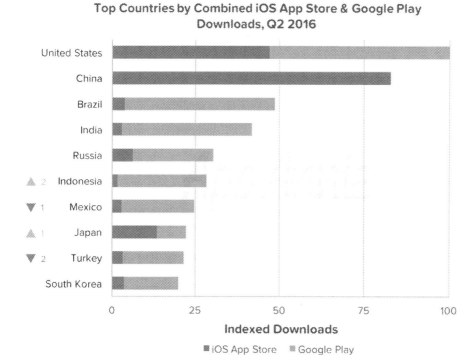

Figure 1-2. Top countries as shown by combined iOS App Store and Google Play downloads, Q2 2016 Source: App Annie Index, Market Q3, 2016

The download rate for iOS apps in China is nearly double the American rate. The Google Play downloads in Brazil and India are nearly as large as the United States.

If you go by revenue, the numbers are slightly different (see Figure 1-3).

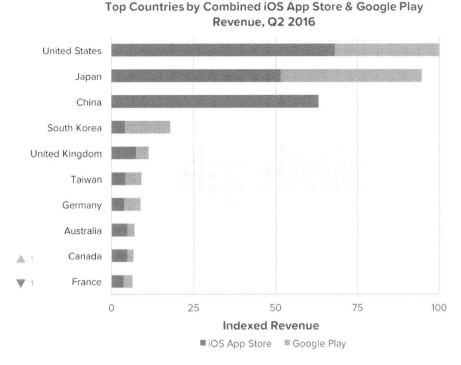

Figure 1-3. *Top countries by combined iOS App Store and Google Play revenue, Q2 2016 Source: App Annie Index, Market Q3 2016*

When measured by revenue instead of downloads, most of the world trails the US market. Japan and China generate close to the same revenue as the US app stores.

The App Annie charts are indexed based on the downloads and revenues of the US markets. The Google Play downloads are not shown for China due to the small market share for Google Play. The Chinese Android app store market has multiple players.

Smartphone users want apps that have been localized to their language. A 2014 survey by Common Sense Advisory queried 3,000 users in 10 countries for which English was not the primary language. The results showed that 75% prefer to buy apps in their native language, and 60% rarely or never purchased English-only apps.

Other Reasons for Localizing an App

You may have legal or contractual obligations to provide localized versions of your application. If you are working on an app as a contractor, you may have specific requirements for language and culture support. If you are doing an app for Canadian customers, for example, they want both English and French supported.

Although you don't have to be fluent in multiple languages, you can make sure that your app can support multiple languages and countries. Even if the language doesn't change, there might be cultural differences. For example, the culture settings have different date formatting between US English, Canadian English, and UK English.

5

Identifying Language and Culture

The standard way of identifying language and country in software development is to use variations of the Internet Engineering Task Force (IETF) language tag to identify language and culture in your code. The IETF is a collection of groups that develop and promote Internet standards. Originally prompted by the US government, the IETF is now an international nonprofit organization.

In 1995, an IETF group called the Network Working Group published RFC 1766: "Tags for the Identification of Languages." It defines the tag used to indicate a language. Although there are variations of the tag definition, the focus here is on the common one- and two-part conventions. The syntax of this tag is the primary tag ("-" subtag). For this book, the tag is referred to as the *language* or *locale string*.

The language codes are typically the two-letter codes from the ISO-639-1 table. Some common entries are shown in Table 1-1.

Table 1-1. *Selected ISO 639-1 Language Codes*

Language name	Native Name	ISO 639-1 Code
English	English	en
Spanish	Español	es
French	Français	fr
Italian	Italiano	it
Japanese	日本語	ja
Russian	Русский	ru
Portuguese	Português	pt
Arabic	العربية	ar
Hindi	हिन्दी	hi
Chinese	中文 (Zhōngwén)	zh
German	Deutsch	de

For script languages, you can use the ISO 15924 standard, which uses a four-letter code. The first letter is uppercase; the remaining three are lowercase. Use this standard if you are supporting both the traditional and simplified forms of the Chinese language. For example, Chinese in the simplified script is designated as zh-Hans, and Chinese in the traditional script is zh-Hant. You can still append the region code after the script code. For simplified Chinese for the Hong Kong region, use zh-Hans-HK.

The subtag represents the region in which the language is being used. The subtag is optional and is prefixed with the "-" character when included. The subtags are defined by the two-letter country codes from the ISO 3166 list. These codes are referred to as the Alpha-2 code (see Table 1-2). There is a three-letter code that is referred to as the Alpha-3 code, but it's not used for the subtag.

Table 1-2. *Sample Entries from the ISO 3166 Alpha-2 List*

Country Name	Alpha-2 Code
United States	US
United Kingdom	GB
Brazil	BR
Portugal	PT
Germany	DE
Spain	ES
Mexico	MS
China	CN
Canada	CA
France	FR

To stay consistent, this book uses the "-" character to separate the tags to stay consistent. Some operating systems (OSs) such as iOS use the underscore ("_") character to separate the language tag from the region tag.

Android needs to have an *r* prefix in the region code for the folder names. For example, Spanish spoken in Mexico needs an Android resource folder defined as es-rMX. In your code, the format of the current locale is referenced through the Resources.Configuration.Locale property that uses an underscore as the separator. For the Spanish in Mexico example, the locale is returned as es_MX.

Although this Android deviation usually doesn't require attention, sometimes you have to remember that the locale strings from Android may need to be manipulated. One such situation occurs when you are requesting localized data from a web service. You want to be able to use a single set of resources to handle all the platforms. (The sample app that you will build in Chapter 3 shows an example of how to do this.)

Most of the time, you will work with the two-part code. By convention, the primary tag is lowercase, and the subtag is uppercase. For example, for US English, the language tag is en-US. For the UK, it is en-GB (see Table 1-3).

Table 1-3. *Some Common Locale Strings*

Country Name	Locale
English, United States	en-US
English, United Kingdom	en-GB
English, Canada	en-CA
French, Canada	fr-CA
French, France	fr-FR
Portuguese, Portugal	pt-PT
Portuguese, Brazil	pt-BR
Chinese (simplified), China	zh-Hans-CN
Chinese (traditional), Hong Kong	zh-Hant-HK
Arabic, Egypt	ar-EG

> ░ **Note** Because a locale string can be in the formats of xx, xx-XX, xx-Xxxx, or xx-Xxxx-XX, try to avoid
> parsing and manipulating the string. With the exception of dealing with Android and the extra r, just pass the
> locale string through and let the runtime pick the right set of resource files.
>
> Prior to iOS 8, iOS supported only the primary tag. You could specify the language, but not the country. If you
> were supporting the French language, you needed to make sure that the words and terms used were common
> to multiple dialects.

When your application starts up, it attempts to match the closest language based on the language string and the resource files included with the application. It tries to find the closest match first, based on the primary tag and subtag. If that search fails, it attempts to locate the resource based on just the primary tag. If that fails, it will just use the default language of the app. (That default is the language that the developer used as the default.)

You don't need to account for every variation of language and culture. If all the English strings in your app are the same across multiple dialects, you just need to provide a single en language resource. If most of the strings are the same, but a few are dialect specific, you can handle that as well. Let's say that the English strings in your app are 99% identical between the US and the UK version; the only difference in this app is the word *color*. In the UK, the preferred spelling is *colour*. You can handle this by putting all the strings in an en resource file. You would then also have an en-GB resource file that contained colour.

With the French language, two of the most popular dialects are the Metropolitan version used in France (fr-FR) and the Canadian version (fr-CA). Canadian French is considered less formal than Metropolitan French; for example, Canadian French uses fewer specifiers and instead uses *que* as a relative pronoun.

For example, for the sentence "I found the document I needed," the Canadian French translation would be "J'ai trouvé le document que j'ai de besoin." The Metropolitan French version would be "J'ai trouvé le document dont j'ai besoin." Another example is the term for *weekend*. In Metropolitan French, you use *le weekend*; in Canadian French, you use *la fin de semaine*.

Portuguese is another language with dialect differences. I'll refer to the dialect spoken in Portugal as European Portuguese. Brazilian Portuguese has grammar rules and nouns that are different from the European Portuguese. Some examples of these differences are shown in Table 1-4.

Table 1-4. *Selected Differences Between Brazilian and European Portuguese*

English	Brazilian Portuguese	European Portuguese
media	mídia	media
train	trem	Comboio
bus	Ônibus	autocarro
brown	marrom	castanho

Be careful when doing partial resource files. Although they take up less space, you have a greater risk of missing some of the translations.

Where Does the Language String Come From?

The language string is supplied to your application from the OS. Although the values that make up both parts of the language string come from ISO 639 and ISO 3166 lists, they don't contain all the values of either list. Most mobiles support a subset of countries and languages. With iOS, Apple supports more than 30 languages for the OS, but the user can select any language and region. Windows 10 for desktop has an extensive set of supported languages. Windows 10 for the phone supports a more limited set of languages, and that list can be limited by the region in which the phone was sold.

The languages supported by a device can vary. Newer versions of an OS usually add more languages. Some vendors may limit the number of languages supported by region.

For the most part, you do not need to do anything with the language string. The runtime code in your application should manage parsing the language string and selecting the right resource file. When you do locale aware formatting, the region code of the language string is used to manage the other part of localization: the formatting of dates, times, numbers, and so on.

░ **Note** Although iOS supports almost any language and region combination, iTunes Connect supports a smaller list of languages. So although your app can be localized in a language like Polish, the app descriptions are not available in Polish; they default to English.

Other Things to Consider

In addition to handling internationalization and localization, you may need to also work with features that are bigger in one market than in others.

Users in China do not have access to Facebook or Twitter. In their place, the popular social media apps in China are WeChat and Weibo. With more than 300 million WeChat users, leveraging the WeChat integration API from your app can provide added exposure to your app.

Which Languages Do You Need to Support?

If you are developing your app in English and you have decided to add support for other languages, you need to decide which languages to add. If you need to support languages X, Y, and Z for contractual obligations, your choices are already defined for you. You can build in the support for the cultural elements and have the text translated by professionals.

If you are large company such as Facebook, you support as many languages as you possibly can. At the time that this book was written, Facebook supports more than 70 languages. It is a large enough company to have its own translation staff.

If you are the software development team or a significant portion of your company's software team, you don't have the same resources available that Facebook has. So you'll need to pick and choose which languages to support. One way to choose languages to support is by the number of native speakers. The top ten languages for native speakers is shown in Table 1-5.

Table 1-5. *Top Ten Languages by Population (2016) Source: Lewis, M. Paul, Gary F. Simons, and Charles D. Fennig (eds.). 2016. Ethnologue: Languages of the World, 19th ed. Dallas, Texas: SIL International*

Rank	Language	Native Speakers (in Millions)
1	Chinese	1,302
2	Spanish	427
3	English	339
4	Arabic	267
5	Hindi	260
6	Portuguese	202
7	Bengali	189
8	Russian	171
9	Japanese	128
10	Lahnda	117

Let's suppose that you wrote your app for just the English language. Your potential audience of native speakers is approximately 340 million. The actual numbers would be a percentage of that 340 million because there are fewer smartphone users. But the number gives you something to work with.

If you add support for just Chinese and Spanish, you expand your potential market from 340 million to a combined total of 2 billion, roughly 5 times the size of your original market. You can't count on every single person being a potential customer, but it does show that Chinese and Spanish speakers greatly outnumber English speakers.

What's Involved with Translation?

When you write an app that will support multiple languages, you have to separate the text and other assets (images, videos, audio) from the code. Having the text strings in a resource file provides two benefits for you.

First, you can have the application framework select the appropriate language resource file at runtime; you don't need the code to pick the correct language. The application runtime will determine the user's current language and culture and will load in the best match for the locale.

The second benefit is to be able to provide just the text resources to a translator. You don't need to provide all your source code—only the resource files containing the text to translate. (Chapter 2 covers the mechanics of how to work with language resource files.)

Text translation involves more than replacing one word or set of words with another. Other languages can have different rules and usages. It's important to be aware of what needs to be translated and how languages are handled differently between cultures.

One language can have multiple dialects or even character sets. For example, the written Chinese language has two standard character sets: traditional and simplified.

Simplified Chinese was instituted by the People's Republic of China (PRC) in the 1950s and '60s. It was based on work started decades earlier. The simplified characters were created by reducing the number of strokes required to create a character and simplifying the number for forms for a character.

After the implementation of simplified Chinese, the term *traditional Chinese* has been used to describe the previous character set. Modern Unicode supports both simplified and traditional character sets.

If you are supporting mainland China (PRC) and Singapore, you need to support simplified Chinese. If you are supporting Taiwan, Hong Kong, and Singapore, you need to support traditional Chinese. Adoption of simplified Chinese has spread in recent years and support of simplified Chinese is needed to make your product salable.

All English-speaking countries have multiple dialects of the English language. Although the dialects are very close, they have terms unique to each culture. US and Australian English uses the term *truck* to refer to what is called a *lorry* in the UK. What an American refers to as a *cell phone*, Australians and Brits call a *mobile phone*.

Translate Sentences, Not Words

Although it's tempting to just translate words and reuse them in multiple places, that process usually doesn't work. Other languages can have rules that may not exist in your language. Although it may seem like an extra expense to translate the same text multiple times, it's better to treat each label in your app separately. You do get some level of reuse with translations: a set of resources that can be reused is called a *translation memory*. The text for the OK button will be the same every time you use it, for example. But you may find that the same label on two screens could get a different translation due to the length of the word or phrase. It may be short enough on one page, but too long on another page, requiring some human guidance to pick an alternate spelling or abbreviation.

For example, let's say you have an upload button and then a dialog that displays a message after the upload has completed. In English, you have two resource strings:

```
"Upload"
"The upload is complete"
```

Although you could build the dialog message string and use the `"Upload"` string, it can fail for other languages. The same strings in Spanish are the following:

```
"Cargar"
"La carga está completa"
```

Upload is used as a verb when it's the button label and then as a noun in the dialog message. When translated into Spanish, the spelling changed between the verb and noun usages.

Dealing with Grammatical Genders

Many languages have grammatical genders; nouns are considered male, female, or neutral (Slavic, Latin, Greek). Some languages have just male and female genders (Romance languages). Other languages combine the male and female as a mixed gender and still have a neutral gender. Other languages do not use a grammatical gender (English, Afrikaans).

The grammatical gender becomes important when sentences are constructed and the noun is determined at runtime, based on some condition. If you were constructing that sentence in pieces, based some action or condition, you would want to make sure that the grammar is correct for each language.

For example, suppose that you have an app that is connected to the user's car and can report the status of the components of the car. Let's assume that there is some code that reports if the car is running or if the lights are on.

In English, it is the following:

```
The lights are XXXX
The engine is XXXX
```

In Spanish, it is the following:

```
Las luces están XXXX
El motor está XXXX
```

In Spanish, the engine of a car has the masculine gender, whereas the lights are considered to be female. There is also a difference with plural words, but you'll dive into pluralization in the next section.

You can deal with the gender rules in two ways. The first way is to work with sentences and treat the entire sentence as a translatable resource string. The other way is to construct the sentence so that text is abbreviated so the definitive articles are not used. For example, consider this text:

```
The doors are unlocked
```

You can leave off the definitive article and display the text this way:

```
Doors are unlocked
```

Or you can display the text as a condition:

```
Doors: Unlocked.
```

Pluralization

The way languages handle plural forms of nouns can vary widely. English has two forms: one of something and then everything else. Other languages have more complicated rules. Asian languages (Chinese, Korean, Japanese, Vietnamese) use only the plural form. Slavic languages typically have three forms, and the rules that define the conditions for each form can vary with the Slavic family.

The simplest way to deal with the plural rules is to display the quantity as a condition:

```
Apples: 4
```

Avoid doing this, however. Your goal is to have an app that feels natural to the user. Chapter 4 will show a way to handle pluralization that respects the plural forms for the locale that the user has set for the device.

Right-To-Left support

Supporting right-to-left (RTL) languages can be a bit tricky. The example app that you will build in this book will use Xamarin.Forms, which (as of version 2) does not support RTL layouts. If you need to support RTL languages such as Arabic, Hebrew, or Farsi, don't use Xamarin.Forms——at least not for the RTL languages.

Xamarin.Android and Xamarin.iOS let you program using the native UI toolkits. Android has had full support for RTL layouts since Android 4.2. If you need RTL support, make 4.2 the minimum version. You can do RTL layouts in older versions, but it's much easier with version 4.2 and up.

To enable RTL support in Android layout files, you have to do the following:

1. Declare in the app manifest file that this app supports RTL mirroring in the view layouts by adding `android:supportRtl="true"` to the `<application>` element.

2. Replace any layout properties that end in *left* or *right* with *start* and *end*. For example, `paddingLeft` would become `paddingStart`. If you need to support Android versions prior to 4.2, you would have both the left/right and the start/end properties.

In iOS, the mirroring of text layout for RTL languages should be handled transparently. This functionality was added in iOS 9. Unless you are using custom controls, you shouldn't have to do anything extra to support the RTL languages.

Windows uses a property named `FlowDirection` to set RTL mirroring. It is set by the current culture of the device; as a developer, you shouldn't have to do anything extra to provide RTL support. If you are using images that have any form of directional bearing, you have to validate those images to make sure that they are still correct on a RTL view. If you have created your own dialogs, you have to verify that the default button placement is correct for a RTL view.

Layout Considerations

When designing a view, try to place the labels above the text or value fields. When the view is rendered as RTL, the controls will still be correctly placed. Doing so also avoids the potential problem of having translated text being much longer than default text.

With Xamarin.Forms, the `StackLayout` control makes it very easy to place the controls in a vertical list. If you are using Xamarin.iOS, the vertical `UIStackView` accomplishes the same task. On Xamarin.Android, the `LinearLayout` with the orientation set to `vertical` allows you to group elements from top to bottom. For Universal Windows Program (UWP), the `StackPanel` layout control flows the controls from top to bottom by default.

Context Is King

When sending text out to be translated, the context is very important. A word or phrase can have multiple meanings, and there may be only a single correct interpretation, based on the usage. This is what separates a professional translation job from a machine translation job.

In US English, the word *trunk* has several meanings; one of them refers to the storage in the back of a car. In UK English, the word *boot* also has multiple meanings; one of them refers to the rear car storage area.

To provide context, you can provide descriptions of the text to be translated. Screenshots of the application running in the default language can also be useful.

A word or term can be short in length in one language and much longer in another language. A skilled translator can suggest an alternative term or an abbreviation that would provide a better fit with the screen layout.

Currency and Numeric Formatting

The .NET Framework has excellent support for handling global numeric formats. The standard numeric format strings handle the differences for the decimal point character and for the thousands separator character. As long as you use the numeric format strings, the numbers will be displayed in the correct format for the current culture.

Use the following code to format a number to be displayed on the screen:

```
var s = String.Format("{0:n}", 1234567.89));
```

Table 1-6 shows the values for the selected locales.

Table 1-6. *Numeric Formatting by Locale*

Locale	Value
en-US (English, United States)	1,234,567.89
en-CA (English, Canada)	1,234,567.89
fr-CA (French, Canada)	1 234 567,89
fr-FR (French, France)	1 234 567,89
pt-PT (Portuguese, Portugal)	1 234 567,89
pt-BR (Portuguese, Brazil)	1.234.567,89
zh-Hans-CN (Chinese [simplified], China)	1,234,567.89
zh-Hant-CN (Chinese [traditional], Hong Kong)	1,234,567.89
ar-EG (Arabic, Egypt)	1,234,567.890

There is also support in the .NET Framework for currency formatting. The C format specifier formats a number using the locale correct character and in the right place. American dollar values have the $ as the prefix to the currency value; European Union countries display the € as a suffix to the value.

Use the following code to format a currency value to be displayed onscreen:

```
var s = String.Format("{0:C}", 4567.89));
```

You see the values for the selected locales shown in Table 1-7.

Table 1-7. *Currency Formatting by Locale*

Locale	Value
en-US (English, United States)	$4,567.89
en-CA (English, Canada)	$4,567.89
fr-CA (French, Canada)	4 567,89$
fr-FR (French, France)	4 567,89 €
pt-PT (Portuguese, Portugal)	4 567,89 €
pt-BR (Portuguese, Brazil)	R$4.567,89
zh-Hans-CN (Chinese [simplified], China)	¥4,567.89
zh-Hant-CN (Chinese [traditional], Hong Kong)	HK$4,567.89
ar-EG (Arabic, Egypt)	4,567.89.ج.م

You have to be very careful when localizing currency values. You can't print a US dollar amount as a Euro value unless you also do a currency exchange lookup to get the current USD-to-Euro exchange rate. If your app has in app purchases (e.g., Apple In App Purchases), use the currency symbol that the App StoreKit API tells them to use.

If you do want to use currency exchange service within your app, there are free and commercial services available. The European Central Bank has a page showing foreign exchange rates against the euro. (Chapter 5 has more information on currency exchange services.)

If you use a currency exchange rate that comes from an outside source, make that clear to app users. Let them know who is providing the exchange rate and how old the data is.

Dates and Time

Date formatting is always culture specific. Although most countries follow the Gregorian calendar, the order of the date fields and the characters used to separate them can vary wildly.

Getting the right date format for display and data entry is very important. When the day part of the date is less than 12, you can't tell whether the date is in the day/month/year format or the month/day/year format by just looking at the date.

If you need to convert a date value to a string to send to a service, your best bet is to the ISO 8601 format. The ISO 8601 standard defines a date as YYYY-MM-DD. If the date is October 1st, 2016, it is represented as 2016-10-01 as an ISO 8601 string.

The ISO 8601 standard for time is hh:mm:ss, where hh is the number of hours since midnight (0-23), mm is the number of minutes (00-59), and ss is the number of seconds (0-60).

▓ **Note**   Seconds can go up to 60 to account for an inserted leap second. Every few years, an extra second is added into the Coordinated Universal Time (UTC) scale, which keeps atomic clocks in sync with the rotation of the earth.

Values containing both time and date just combine the two formats as YYYY-MM-DDThh:mm:ss. Case matters: MM and mm have two different meanings. The former is the number of the month; the latter is the number of minutes.

The .NET Framework has standard patterns for formatting date and time strings. The "d" format string formats the date using the ShortDatePattern. When you use the date and time format strings, the .NET Framework returns string values using the correct field order and date and/or time separators. Let's take a look at some code and see how the date formatting changes for different cultures:

```
var dt = new DateTime(2016, 10, 2);

System.Threading.Thread.CurrentThread.CurrentCulture = new CultureInfo("en-US");

Console.WriteLine("English (US)");
Console.WriteLine(dt.ToString("D"));
Console.WriteLine(dt.ToString("d"));
Console.WriteLine(dt.ToString("s"));

System.Threading.Thread.CurrentThread.CurrentCulture = new CultureInfo("pt-BR");

Console.WriteLine("\nPortuguese (Brazil)");
Console.WriteLine(dt.ToString("D"));
Console.WriteLine(dt.ToString("d"));
Console.WriteLine(dt.ToString("s"));

System.Threading.Thread.CurrentThread.CurrentCulture = new CultureInfo("de-GR");

Console.WriteLine("\nGerman (Germany)");
Console.WriteLine(dt.ToString("D"));
Console.WriteLine(dt.ToString("d"));
Console.WriteLine(dt.ToString("s"));
```

When you run that code, you get the following output:

```
English (US)
Sunday, October 2, 2016
10/2/2016
2016-10-02T00:00:00

Portuguese (Brazil)
domingo, 2 de outubro de 2016
02/10/2016
2016-10-02T00:00:00

German (Germany)
Sonntag, 2. Oktober 2016
02.10.2016
2016-10-02T00:00:00
```

The Long Date ("D") format shows that punctuation, spelling, and case will change based on the culture. The Short Date ("d") format shows how the ordering of the date fields and the date field separator changes. The Sortable ("s") format string follows the ISO 8601 standard, and the result is the same for each culture.

When working with multiple time zones or dealing with multiple calendars, consider using the Noda Time library (http://nodatime.org/). It has code conversions from one time zone to another and code for converting dates from the default calendar to other calendars, such as the Hebrew, Islamic, and Coptic calendars.

Capitalization

When translating text, the professional translator should be aware of the capitalization rules for the language that is being translated to. Here are a couple of example rules:

- English and German capitalize days of the week, month names, and language names. With other languages, the rules vary, but most do not capitalize days of the week or months.

- In German and Luxembourgish (a German-derived language), all nouns are capitalized. Most European languages capitalize single word nouns, and multiple word nouns follow English publication rules (such as "Cooking for Fun").

Sorting

The same set of characters can sort one way in one language and have a subtly different order in another language. With some languages, a sequence of letters is treated as a different character for sorting. In the Czech language, the letter pair of *ch* comes after the letter *h*, but any other combination using the letter *c* follows the letter c. Consider the list of names shown in Table 1-8.

Table 1-8. *Comparison of Sort Orders*

Sort Order	Sorted with English Culture	Sorted with Czech Culture
1	Carl	Carl
2	Charles	Harrison
3	Harrison	Charles
4	James	James

If you sort the data on the device with a .Net Framework method such as List<T>.Sort(), the Sort() method should sort the values using a collation sequence that is correct in the current culture. If you download a list from a web service and that service has sorted the list, it may not be in the right order if that web service is running on a machine with different culture settings.

There are a couple of ways to ensure that you have your data sorted correctly. One way is to have the web service sort the data using the culture information from the device. If the web service uses a List<T>.Sort(), there is an overload to the Sort() method that lets you pass in a culture specific compared with the sort method.

Staying with the Czech example, consider the case of a user using a device set to the Czech language and culture, and an app is requesting a sorted user list from an English web server. When the app makes the request for the user list, somewhere in the web service request the locale string of cs-CZ (Czech [Czech Republic]) is passed in. The web service could use a syntax like the following to pass back a locale-specific sorted list:

```
Userlist.Sort(StringComparer.Create(new CultureInfo(LocaleString), true));
```

This code would perform a cases-insensitive sort on UserList with the locale stored in the variable named LocaleString.

The other way to ensure a locale-correct sort sequence is to sort the data on the device after making the web service call to get the list.

Images

If your app makes extensive use of images, you may need to localize some of them. When using images for icons, you want to make sure that the image has meaning for the cultures that you are supporting.

Try to avoid using country flags to indicate a culture. If you use a French flag to indicate some setting when the app is running with the French language, you will offend Francophone users in Quebec. Québécois is a distinct version of the French language, and its speakers have a strong identification with their culture.

If your app uses a custom color palette, you need to be aware that your color choice may have an unintended significance in other countries. Be careful with images or symbology used with the color. For example, don't use a book icon in the color yellow for the Chinese market. In Chinese culture, *yellow book* is a term for pornographic material.

If you are providing video and/or audio content, they may need to changed or updated to include subtitles. If the images are part of the layout, you need to verify that they look correct on an RTL layout.

Input Validation

If you are using entry validation, you want to avoid having validation rules that require a minimum number of characters. A single kanji is sufficient for a name in some languages. In Indonesia, it's still common for individuals of Javanese descent to have only a single name, or *mononym*. In Burma, mononyms are common. The third Secretary General of the United Nations was *U Thant*. *Thant* is his name; *U* is the Burmese equivalent of *Mr*.

Most Icelanders have a single name, and they may use a patronymic or matronymic in lieu of a surname. For example, the Icelandic musician Björk uses the patronym Guðmundsdóttir to indicate that she is the daughter of Guðmundur Gunnarsson. If she used your app, she would probably just want to use *Björk* for the name field.

When you allow number entry, make sure that your validation code correctly detects decimal marks and thousands separators.

Whenever possible, use the `datetime` picker controls to get the date and time into the correct formats.

App Store Material

In addition to the text assets used in your application, you should also have the metadata translated that gets sent to the app stores. This metadata can include short and long descriptions, images, videos, and support contact information. The specific information required will depend on the store to which you are submitting the app.

It's important to localize the app store data. When a user searches for an app, you want the localized version of your app showing up in the app store search listings. App stores often require a privacy policy URL and e-mail addresses for support. You should have fully localized versions of your privacy policy and be ready to provide support in the languages that your app supports.

How to Get Your Text Translated

A fast and inexpensive way to translate your text is to use machine translation. Both Microsoft and Google have translation tools that are pretty good. But they are not perfect, and they won't understand the context of your application. You could have a sentence in English that could be translated four different ways into Spanish. Each translation might be grammatically correct, but only one of them is the right translation for you.

Machine translation does provide some good value. It's a great way to make sure that all your text assets in the app are represented as translatable resources. If you have an app that was translated into Spanish and you run the app and see the words Place Order, you know that you missed that text. Human translators can use machine translation tools to do the bulk of the work. They can then review the translations and correct the translated text as needed.

The other immediate advantage of machine translation is checking to make sure that the text fits in the screen layout. Some languages are more verbose than others. If your app was laid out so that all the text is squeezed in, you'll probably have some problems when running under other cultures. Use a layout that places labels above text entry or value fields to avoid problems with the lengths changing.

Machine translations are no substitute for professional translations. You want your apps to have a natural feel and not have any jarring translation miscues. Professional-looking apps always have human translation and/or review of machine-translated text.

If your company has inhouse translation resources, it is a great advantage. You have people with the domain knowledge of the apps and have the context to understand the needs for text usage in the app. Unless it's a formal translation department, the odds are that you will get the translation work done without a significant budget cost to you.

You may also have access to local language professionals who might be willing to take on some translation work. Your local university or high school may have staff that can do some translating. It will take some extra work on your part to make sure that the translator knows the context of text from your app.

And there are companies that provide professional translation services. If you need to have translation performed in multiple languages, a professional service can provide the languages that you need and can usually get the job done in less time than someone doing it as a side job.

For the sample app in Chapter 3, a company named SmartCat.AI did some volunteer work to translate the small amount of text needed for the app. SmartCat provides a nice workflow that works well with application development.

For a commercial app, the translation workflow works something like this:

1. Register for an account on SmartCat.ai.

2. Create a new project and upload the assets to be translated. Professional translation houses can handle files in many formats.

3. Search for available translators for the languages that you need translated. SmartCAT works with freelance translators. You can pick the translator with the experience that best matches the text to be translated. You can filter the list by experience and rates.

4. Select the translator; if the translator takes on the job, that person starts working on your assets. SmartCAT provides a web portal, and you can access the translations as they are performed.

5. Review the translated resources, and the work is completed. SmartCAT then arranges for the payment to the translator.

Other services have different workflows. You may see a workflow in which you get a project manager assigned to your app. You would provide the text assets to the product manager, and that manager works with people to get the material translated.

Many of these companies are used to mobile app development needs and can work with you to make sure that the additional items for the app store are met. You can expect to pay anywhere from $0.10 to $0.25 per word (at the time of writing) with a professional translation company.

CHAPTER 2

■ ■ ■

Working with Resource Files

Coffee is also a language in itself.

—Jackie Chan, Chinese Radio International, June 2006

About File Formats

When it comes to managing string resources for localization purposes, there are some file formats that you will need to work with. Applications written with the .NET Framework make use of the RESX file format. Xamarin.Android applications can also use the native Android `strings.xml` file. Apps written with Xamarin. iOS can use the native `LocalizedString` files. To manage language resource files for use with translation professionals, you can import and export XLIFF files.

The tools that Visual Studio provides do a great job of letting you concentrate on the text translations. It is helpful to know a little bit about the underlying file structures.

RESX

The RESX file format is the string resource file format used by the .NET Framework. A `.resx` resource file contains objects and strings enclosed inside XML tags.

Visual Studio provides designers for the `.resx` files. It also provides a table structure to make it easy for the developer to add and modify string resources. Using XML as the file format makes it easy to provide tooling for working with the `.resx` files.

When you add a `.resx` file to your project, Visual Studio also adds a code-behind file that has the same name as the `.resx` file, but with a `.designer.cs` extension. When you build your application, Visual Studio invokes the `resgen.exe` tool to convert the resources defined in the `.resx` XML file into a class that compiles into your application. This class lets you reference the resource text strings as .NET properties, and you get full IntelliSense for picking the text values.

The `.designer.cs` file is generated from the `.resx` file at build time. You should never manually edit the `.designer.cs` file because the changes would be lost the next time you edited the `.resx` file or did a rebuild.

The way to support multiple languages with `.resx` files is straightforward. The default language has a file with the resource name and the `.resx` extension. For example, let's say the resource file is named `MyText.resx`. In that `.resx` file, three string values are defined: Name, Age, and Eye Color.

■ **Note**   A common practice is to add a folder named `Resources` to the project and then place all the `.resx` files inside that folder. For a larger project, doing so keeps things tidy.

© Christopher Miller 2017

C. Miller, *Cross-platform Localization for Native Mobile Apps with Xamarin*,

DOI 10.1007/978-1-4842-2466-3_2

To add the resource file, right-click the project name and select Add and then New Item (see Figure 2-1). If you want the .resx file inside a folder, right-click the folder instead of the project name.

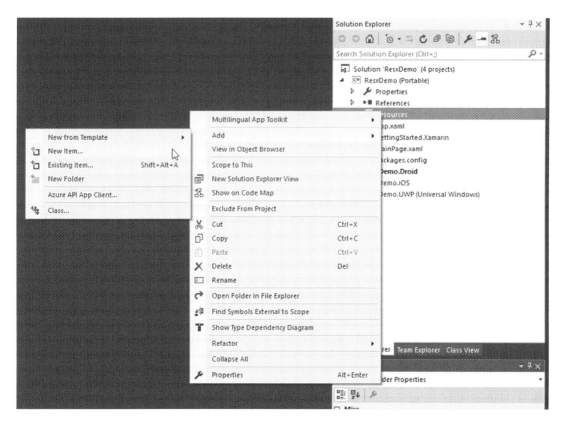

Figure 2-1. *Adding a new item in a Visual Studio project*

When the Add New Item dialog comes up, select Resources File and add your resource file (see Figure 2-2).

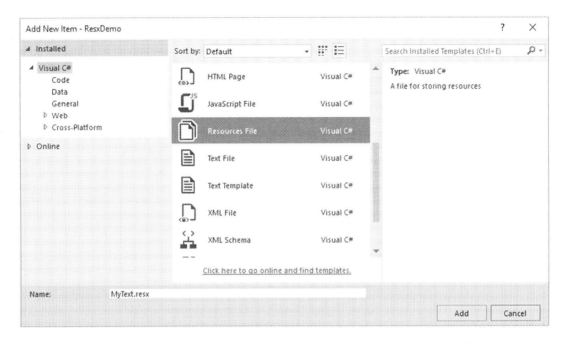

Figure 2-2. *Selecting the Resources File template*

This process creates both the MyText.resx and MyText.Designer.cs files. It then opens up the Resource Designer on the .resx file. The empty resource file should look something like Figure 2-3.

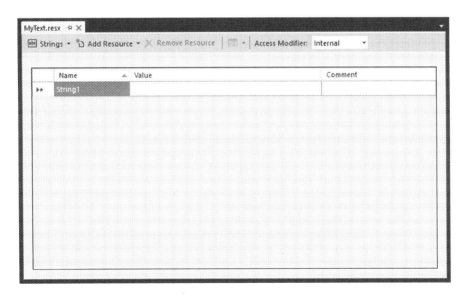

Figure 2-3. *Editing a new .resx file*

The first to change is the `Access Modifier` property. By default, it is set to `Internal`, and only classes within the same project and namespace can access the properties. When you are targeting multiple platforms and sharing the code, you want the resources defined in the shared code as much as possible. So change the `Access Modifier` from `Internal` to `Public`.

Add the string values to be used in the app in a table format, as shown in Figure 2-4. The name of the string value is what is exposed as code, so the name has to follow the same rules as any other property. After adding the `Name`, `Age`, and `EyeColor` strings, you should see something similar to Figure 2-4.

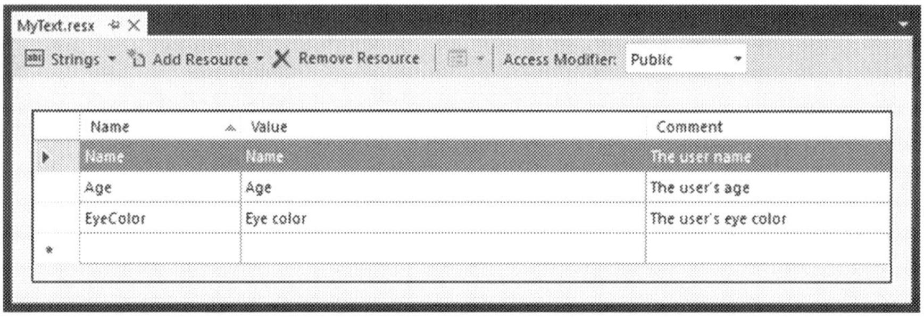

Figure 2-4. *The .resx file with text values defined*

Once you save the `.resx` file, the `.designer.cs` file updates. If you open up the `.designer.cs` file, you'll see some code for managing the resource and then properties defined for each text string. For the `EyeColor` string, the following code is generated:

```
/// <summary>
///     Looks up a localized string similar to Eye color.
/// </summary>
public static string EyeColor {
        get {
                return ResourceManager.GetString("EyeColor", resourceCulture);
        }
}
```

▓ **Note**   You never want to edit the code that appears in the `.designer.cs` file. The code is generated every time you edit the `.resx` file. If you make any manual changes to the `.designer.cs` file, they are lost the next time you edit the `.resx` file.

The process works this way: when you reference a resource string at runtime, it does a lookup based on the current language and country settings (i.e., the locale). If it finds a match for that locale, it uses that set of string resources. If it can't match that locale, it tries to match on just the language. If that fails, the default resource file is used.

When you add resource files for additional languages, they get a `.designer.cs` file, but not the autogenerated properties. The code defined for the default language will be used for the additional languages.

Because you created a `.resx` resource named `MyText`, it will be the class name for your string resources. If the `.resx` file is created in a folder, it has the folder name as part of its namespace.

To reference the string resource in code, use a syntax like this:

```
eyeLabel.Text = MyText.EyeColor;
```

In an XAML page, use something like this:

```
<TextBlock Text="{x:Static MyText.EyeColor}" />
```

With the strongly typed resource file, you get full IntelliSense as you are typing (this applies to both the code-behind .cs file and with the XAML page). And you get compile time validation that the resource has been defined. If you remove or rename a string resource, the code will fail to compile, and the compiler errors will show where the string resources were previously referenced.

To add a second language, just add a new resource file and name the file with the language (and culture, if used). To add Spanish, you can add a resource file named MyText.es.resx. Now you can define the same strings that were defined for the default language.

This set of translated strings work for any locale (language + country) that uses Spanish. To use Spanish in Spain, the locale code is es-ES; to use Spanish in Mexico, the locale string is es-MX. Users in both locales get the same translated results.

If you want to support a language for multiple countries, you can create a .resx file for each language/country combination. The Portuguese language has two popular dialects. European Portuguese is used in the country of Portugal, and Brazilian Portuguese is the dialect used in the county of Brazil. To create the resource file for European Portuguese, the locale code is pt-PT, where the lowercase *pt* is the language code and the uppercase *PT* is the country code. For Brazil, use the same language code and replace the country code with the code for Brazil, which is *BR*, defining the local code as pt-BR. You can then create the resource files as MyText.pt-PT.resx and MyText.pt-BR.resx. Table 2-1 shows examples of file names by locale.

Table 2-1. *Some Sample RESX File Names by Locale*

Language (and Country)	Folder Name
Spanish	MyText.es.resx
Spanish (Mexico)	MyText.es-MX.resx
Spanish (Spain)	MyText.es-ES.resx
Portuguese	MyText.pt.resx
Portuguese (Portugal)	MyText.pt-PT.resx
Portuguese (Brazil)	MyText.pt-BR.resx
Chinese (Traditional) (Taiwan)	MyText.zh-Hant-TW.resx
Chinese (Simplified) (PRC)	MyText.zh-Hans-CN.resx
Japanese	MyText.ja.resx

▨ **Note**   To quickly copy the string values from the default .resx file to the additional language file, open the .resx file in the designer. Select all the rows with the mouse, right-click on the rows, and select Copy. Open the new .resx file in the designer, right-click in the designer, and select Paste. This process copies all names, values, and comments. Now you can just edit the values.

Now you can enter the Spanish translations of the English text. These terms are simple enough, so they can be translated with either the Microsoft or Google online services. Once the text is translated, the .resx file should look like Figure 2-5.

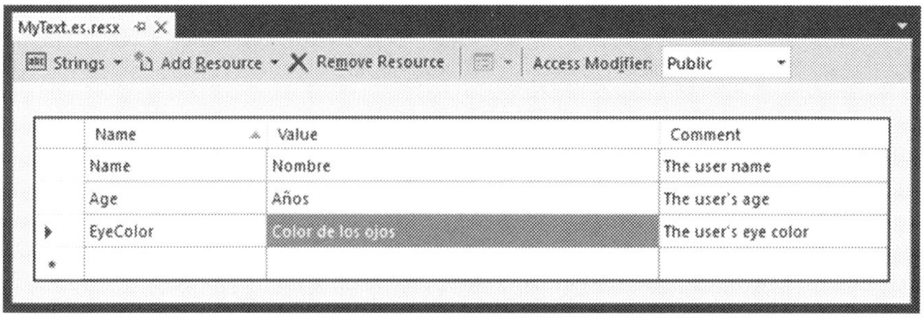

Figure 2-5. *Spanish translated version of the .resx file*

Here, a one-for-one translation was done. If the second language shares the same value for some of the strings in the default language, you have to translate only the ones with different values. For example, in the UK, the word *color* is spelled as *colour*, and you can make a .resx for that culture.

Add the new .resx as MyText.en-GB.resx, which designates the resource as having the English language and the locale as the United Kingdom. When that resource file opens up in the designer, add only the EyeColor string resource (see Figure 2-6).

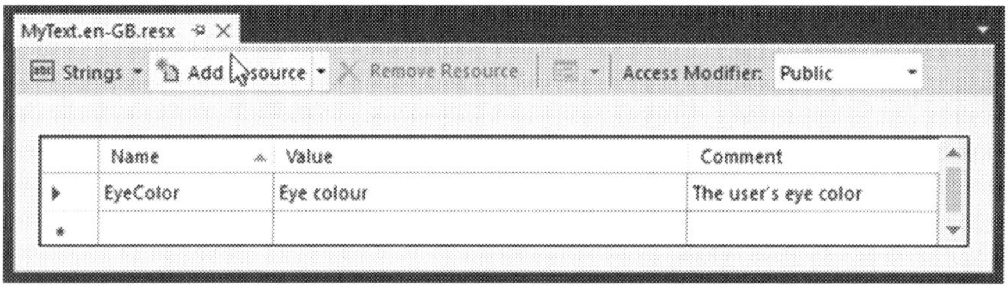

Figure 2-6. *Example of a partially translated .resx file*

If the app were running as UK English, at runtime the EyeColor resource property would find a match in the en-GB resource file and come back with Eye colour. Referencing the Age property would not find a match with the en-GB resource file and would fall back to the next closest match. In this case, it would be the default resource, and Age would be returned.

░ **Note** If you define some string resources in a shared library and you can't access them from another project, double-check the Access Modifier property and make sure it is set to Public.

Android XML

Android apps have their own string resource format that is XML based. By convention, the file is named `strings.xml` and it is located in the `res/values` folder for the Android project. Xamarin Android apps use the same files, but the folder location is `Resources/values`.

To create an Android string resource file that has the same strings as the RESX example, the file should look like this:

```
<?xml version="1.0" encoding="utf-8"?>
<resources>
  <string name="Name">Name</string>
  <string name="Age">Age</string>
  <string name="EyeColor">Eye Color</string>
</resources>
```

To add additional language support, add a new `strings.xml` file, but in a `values` folder that has the language and culture as the suffix (separated by a dash (`-`)). So for the Spanish example, there can be a `strings.xml` file in the `Resources/values-es` folder that looks like this:

```
<?xml version="1.0" encoding="utf-8"?>
<resources>
  <string name="Name">Nombre</string>
  <string name="Age">Años</string>
  <string name="EyeColor">Color de los ojos</string>
</resources>
```

This resource file uses *es* to match all Spanish language users. To match by country and language, add *-r* and the country code. To go with the Portuguese examples, the folder names for European Portuguese and Brazilian Portuguese are `values-pt-rPT` and `values-pt-rBR`, respectively.

As with the `.resx` files, if you leave off a string translation, the resource engine looks for the closest match. The UK `strings.xml` file would be located in the `Resources/values-en-rGB` folder:

```
<?xml version="1.0" encoding="utf-8"?>
<resources>
  <string name="EyeColor">Eye Colour</string>
</resources>
```

Android prefixes the country or region code with an *r* character. The codes are not case sensitive, but the convention is to use a lowercase language code and an uppercase region code. Remember to use the *r*; otherwise, Android will reject that resource folder. Some example folder names are shown in Table 2-2.

Table 2-2. *Select Android Values Folder Names by Locale*

Language (and Country)	Folder name
Spanish	values-es
Spanish (Mexico)	values-es-rMX
Spanish (Spain)	values-es-rES
Portuguese	values-pt
Portuguese (Brazil)	values-pt-rBR
Chinese (Traditional) (Taiwan)	values-zh-rTW
Chinese (Simplified) (PRC)	values-zh-rCN
Japanese	values-ja

▒ **Note** If you are running an Android emulator, it has an app installed named Custom Locale. If you run that app, you can see all the supported languages and locales for that version of Android.

There are two ways to use a string resource in Android. In an Android view, you can use syntax like the following:

```
<Button
    android:id="@+id/myButton"
    android:layout_width="fill_parent"
    android:layout_height="wrap_content"
    android:text="@string/EyeColor"
    />
```

In code, use the GetString() method:

```
eyeLabel.Text = context.Resources.GetString(Resource.String.EyeColor);
```

As with the .resx file, this will provide IntelliSense matching and compile time validation for the string resource value. If you misspell *EyeColor* as *EYEColor*, it will fail to compile.

Although Xamarin.Android does work in the native strings.xml format, it's easier to use the .NET .resx files when working with multiple platforms with shared code.

Apple iOS String Dictionary

With iOS, Apple uses a different mechanism for localizing string resources. Instead of an XML-based storage format, Apple uses key-value pairs, and the default name of the file is Localizable.strings (but you can use any valid file name). The location is in an xx.lproj folder, where xx is the name of the language (and region, if used). If English is your default language, you will have a string resource file named Localizable.strings in a folder named en.lproj. (See Table 2-3 for some examples of names by locale.)

Table 2-3. *Sample iOS Localizable.strings Names by Locale*

Language (and Country)	Folder Name
Spanish	es.lproj/Localizable.strings
Spanish (Mexico)	es-MX.lproj/Localizable.strings
Spanish (Spain)	es-ES.lproj/Localizable.strings
Portuguese	pt.lproj/Localizable.strings
Portuguese (Brazil)	pt-BR.lproj/Localizable.strings
Chinese (Traditional)	zh-Hant.lproj/Localizable.strings
Chinese (Simplified)	zh-Hans.lproj/Localizable.strings
Japanese	ja.lproj/Localizable.strings

▓ **Note** Versions of iOS prior to iOS 7 supported only language localization files. In iOS 7, region codes were added.

Using the `.resx` and `string.xml` examples from the RESX and Android examples, the Name/Age/EyeColor strings look like this:

```
/* The user name */
"Name"="Name";
/* The user's age */
"Age"="Age";
/* The user's eye color */
"EyeColor"="Eye Color";
```

It's important that the code-like syntax is correct. The code will not load if you are missing a semicolon at the end of the line. If your string has an embedded newline, it has to escaped with a "\n". (The double quotes and backslash characters also must be escaped.)

There are a few differences between the way iOS handles resource string names and the way Android and .NET handle them. Because Apple is using key-value pairs, the resource name can be any valid string. (You could have used `Eye color` for the string name instead of `EyeColor`).

With iOS, resource files get compiled into what is referred to as the Application bundle. With Xamarin.iOS, you use the `LocalizedString()` method from the main bundle of the app to reference a string. To access a string resource with Xamarin.iOS, you can use syntax like this:

```
eyeLabel.Text = NSBundle.MainBundle. LocalizedString("EyeColor", "");
```

This code returns the localized value for `"EyeColor"`. If a string resource for `"EyeColor"` does not exist, the value `"EyeColor"` is returned. The second parameter is a placeholder for a comment, which is a hint to a translator for the context of this string.

C# makes that access code a little simpler and easier to read. A string extension posted by Thomas Rosenstein on Stackoverflow.com adds a method named t() to all strings. The following code was based on code originally posted on the Stackoverflow site (http://stackoverflow.com/a/6270189/206):

```
public static class Extension
{
    public static string t(this string translate)
    {
        return NSBundle.MainBundle.LocalizedString(translate, string.Empty);
    }
}
```

With that extension, the previous line of code can be written as follows:

```
eyeLabel.Text = "EyeColor".t();
```

Xamarin.iOS can use either the Localizable.strings resources or the .NET .resx files. As with Android, if you are sharing code across platforms, it's easier to use .resx files.

▓ **Note**   With the iOS LocalizedString() method, there is no compile time validation that the resource has been defined. If you misspell the name of the resource, it will compile without any errors and it will just use the resource name as the value of that resource.

CHAPTER 3

▒ ▒ ▒

Working with Multilingual App Toolkit

I have a thing for tools.

—Tim Allen

Multilingual App Toolkit

Microsoft has a very handy tool for working with language translation files: the Multilingual App Toolkit, or MAT for short. It is an extension for Visual Studio 2013 and Visual Studio 2015.

The MAT provides the following functionality:

- It integrates with Visual Studio and becomes part of the workflow. It adds and manages translation files using the standard Visual Studio IDE. It works almost any Visual Studio project that uses `.resx` resource files.

- It provices seudo language support, which is used during testing. It allows you to find places in the application in which the localization is incomplete. The problem might be missing translations, translations that don't fit, or other problems. The pseudo language appears as another XLIFF file and can be edited as with any other language.

- It provides machine language translation for many (but not all) languages. The translation is provided through the Microsoft Translator service.

- The translation files are stored in XLIFF 1.2 and can be used to send and receive resources to third-party translation services.

- It comes with a dedicated editor to easily edit and view translated text strings. By using the standard XLIFF state and state-qualifier attributes, a basis workflow can be used to manage the translation process. (More information about the XLIFF file format can be found in Chapter 5.)

© Christopher Miller 2017
C. Miller, *Cross-platform Localization for Native Mobile Apps with Xamarin*,
DOI 10.1007/978-1-4842-2466-3_3

Installation

There are a couple of ways to install the MAT. From within Visual Studio, you can install it by performing the following steps:

1. From the Tools menu, select Extensions and Updates. The Extensions and Updates dialog displays, which lets you install and update various addins for Visual Studio.

2. In the panel on the left side of the dialog, click Online. You see a list all available extensions that can be installed.

3. In the search box located in the upper-right corner of the dialog, type **multilingual**. This process filters the list of extensions and should show Multilingual App Toolkit at the top of the list (see Figure 3-1). At the time of this writing, version 4 is the latest edition.

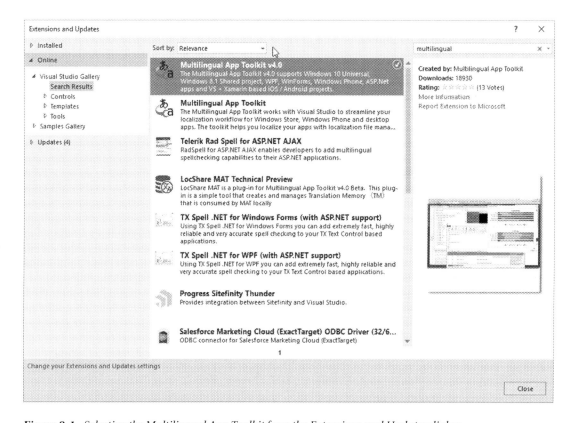

Figure 3-1. *Selecting the Multilingual App Toolkit from the Extensions and Updates dialog*

4. Select the Multilingual App Toolkit, making sure to get the latest version. A download button lights up.

5. Press the download button and follow the prompts to download and install the MAT. Restart Visual Studio if prompted do so.

Another way to download and install the MAT is from the Visual Studio Gallery page. Follow these steps:

1. Shut down Visual Studio if it running.

2. With a web browser, go to `https://visualstudiogallery.msdn.microsoft.com/`.

3. In the Find search box, enter **Multilingual App Toolkit** and press Enter. The same list of extensions that was displayed from within Visual Studio is shown. Select the one labelled Multilingual App Toolkit v4.0 (or newer), which brings up the same extension that was displayed within Visual Studio, but with additional information. You can see reviews and a Q&A section.

4. Press the download button to download the installer for the Multilingual App Toolkit. It will be in the `.MSI` format.

5. After downloading the `.MSI` file, open up the folder that contains it. Right-click on the file and select Install.

6. Restart Visual Studio.

Using the MAT

Using the MAT is pretty straightforward. You create an app, put your text in a `.resx` resource file, enable the MAT, translate the text, test it, and finally ship it. To illustrate this process, you'll create a very simple "Hello World" app by using Xamarin.Forms.

This app is a very simple one that shows how to use the resource files and how to change the language at runtime. Setting the language at runtime is different in UWP than it is with Xamarin.Android and Xamarin.iOS. You can use the Xamarin.Forms `DependencyService` to call platform-specific functionality from the shared codes.

The app displays a label and, with the tap of a button, you can change the language of the label from English, to Spanish, and then to Chinese.

Being able to change the language at runtime is a great tool to have at your disposal because you can quickly test different languages without having to force the device or emulator into another language. The author once changed his Windows Phone at a conference into another language and could not read the other language to set it back to English. Fortunately for the author, one of the MAT developers was at the same conference and had the same phone. By comparing the phones side by side, the author could find the language setting and was able to use his phone again.

Start up Visual Studio and create a new project. Select the Blank Xaml App (Xamarin.Forms Portable) template, which creates a solution with multiple projects, one for each target platform. Plus one more project that will contain the shared code as Portable Class Library (PCL). You can do this with a Shared Asset Library, but you'll use PCL for this example. The New Project dialog should look like Figure 3-2.

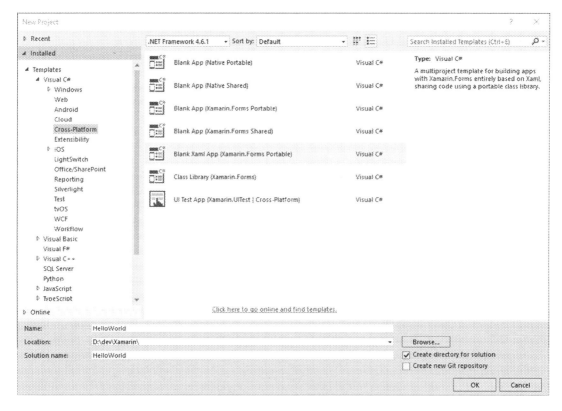

Figure 3-2. *Selecting the Blank XAML Xamarin.Forms Portable template*

This demo will be named HelloWorld, but you can name it anything you like.

After some churning and perhaps a prompt about connecting to a Mac or Windows 10 Target version, you get a Xamarin.Forms solution with multiple projects. It looks similar to Figure 3-3.

Figure 3-3. *Solution Explorer shows the files created by the Blank XAML Xamarin.Forms template*

The first thing that to do is edit the `MainPage.xaml` file. This page contains the XAML needed to render the page. The default code in that page should look something like this:

```xml
<?xml version="1.0" encoding="utf-8" ?>
<ContentPage xmlns="http://xamarin.com/schemas/2014/forms"
xmlns:x="http://schemas.microsoft.com/winfx/2009/xaml"
            xmlns:local="clr-namespace:HelloWorld"
            x:Class="HelloWorld.MainPage">

  <Label Text="Welcome to Xamarin Forms!"
         VerticalOptions="Center"
         HorizontalOptions="Center" />
</ContentPage>
```

You will make a few changes to this XAML file: replace the default label with a new label and some buttons. Replace the `Label` control with the following:

```xml
<StackLayout>
  <StackLayout Orientation="Horizontal">
    <Button x:Name="BtnEnglish" Text="English"/>
    <Button x:Name="BtnSpanish" Text="Spanish"/>
    <Button x:Name="BtnChinese" Text="Chinese"/>
  </StackLayout>
  <Label Text="Welcome to Xamarin Forms!" x:Name="LabelWelcome"
```

```
            VerticalOptions="Center"
            HorizontalOptions="Center" />
</StackLayout>
```

The top-level `StackLayout` container organizes the controls from top to bottom. The first control in the `StackLayout` is another `StackLayout` container, which uses a horizontal layout and arranges its child controls from left to right.

Inside the inner `StackLayout` are three button controls. To keep this example simple, you can assign click event handlers for the buttons at runtime. To do so, you have to assign the `Name` property of each control.

After the inner `StackLayout`, a `Label` control is defined. Now you can add the resource files for the language translation. Create a resources folder to keep the project neat and tidy. Then add a resource file named `MainPageText.resx` to the resources folder. Edit the `.resx` file to include a string resource named `Welcome` (see Figure 3-4).

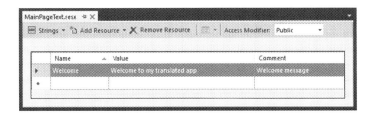

Figure 3-4. *Resource file with the string value that will be localizede*

Save that `.resx` file. Now you can enable the MAT for the shared code project. From the Tools menu, select Multilingual App Toolkit and then Enable selection, as shown in Figure 3-5.

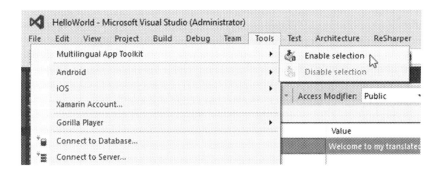

Figure 3-5. *Enabling the MAT*

With the MAT enabled, you can add some languages to the project. From the Project menu, select Multilingual App Toolkit and then choose Add Translation Languages (see Figure 3-6).

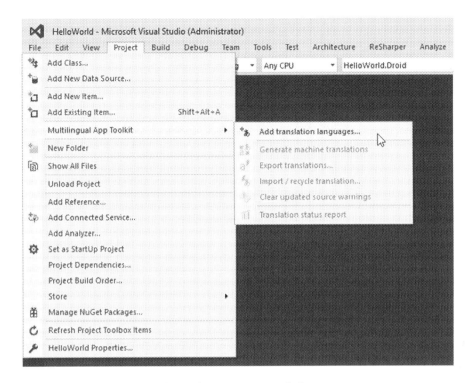

Figure 3-6. *Invoking the Add Translation Languages dialog*

You see a dialog that lists all the languages that are supported, as shown in Figure 3-7. Many of the languages will have translation providers listed to the left of the language name. Languages that have providers available can be machine translated by the MAT.

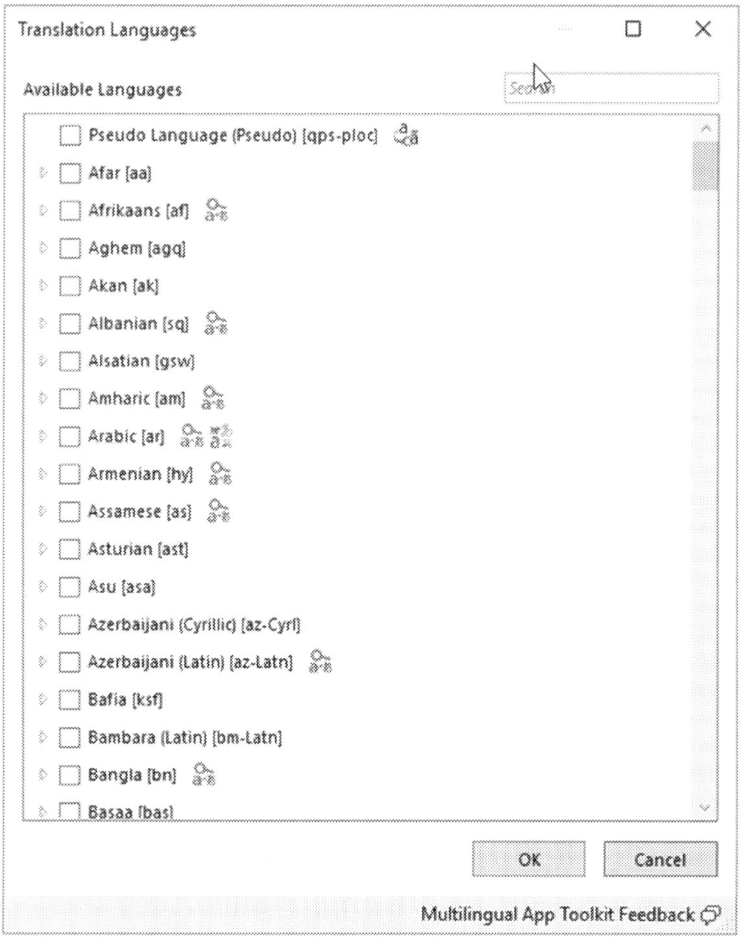

Figure 3-7. *Translation Languages dialog*

There are two providers available. The first one, Microsoft Language Portal Provider, makes use of the professionally translated strings from Microsoft products. The second provider is the Microsoft Translator Provider, which uses Microsoft Translations Services (the same engine that the web site translate.bing. com uses.

Select the Spanish (es) and Chinese (Simplified) (zh-Hans) languages and press OK. The MAT creates two XLIFF 1.2 files in a MultilingualResources folder, one for each language. You should have a HelloWorld.es.xlf and a HellowWorld.zh-Hans.xlf file (see Figure 3-8).

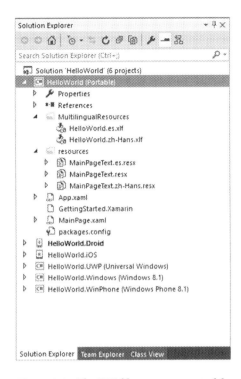

Figure 3-8. *The XLF files are now part of the solution*

To keep the demo simple, you can delete the Windows 8.1 and Windows Phone 8.1 projects because the Android, iOS, and UWP projects are sufficient to show how resource files work. Right-click the Windows 8.1 and Windows Phone 8.1 projects and select Remove.

Have the MAT machine translate the English string resource to Spanish and Chinese. Right-click the `MultilingualResources` folder, select Multilingual App Toolkit and then choose Generate Machine Translations. A progress dialog displays as each of the `.xlf` files is translated (see Figure 3-9).

Figure 3-9. *Progress is updated as each .xlf file is machine translated*

You can view the `.xlf` files with the Multilingual Editor that is part of the MAT. Select the `HellowWorld.es.xlf` file in Solution Explorer. The default action when you double-click the file is to open the `.xlf` file inside Visual Studio. That brings the file in as code and you'll see it in all its XML glory. To get the Multilingual Editor, right-click the file and select Open With. You should see a list of Visual Studio file editors with Multilingual Editor in the list.

If you don't see Multilingual Editor in the list, click the >Add button. Under Program, add the following:

```
"%ProgramFiles%\Multilingual App Toolkit\MultilingualEditor.exe"
```

Under Friendly Name, enter **Multilingual Editor**. Then click OK. You now have Multilingual Editor as an option when you select Open With for the .xlf files.

After the .xlf file opens in the Multilingual Editor, you should see something similar to Figure 3-10.

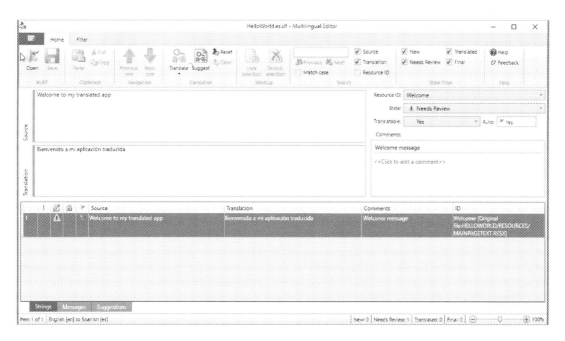

Figure 3-10. *Multilingual Editor*

The Multilingual Editor provides an easy-to-use interface for the XML content stored in the .xlf file. It shows the resource ID, default language version of the text, and translated text. The bottom part of the editor is a grid that lists all the resource strings in the .xlf file. This example app only has a single resource string, so the contents of the grid match the contents in the entry fields.

Because the text was just machine translated, the State field is set to Needs Review. If you click the State field, you can set the set of values that can be selected (see Figure 3-11).

Figure 3-11. *Setting the state of the translated string resource*

Depending on workflow, you can change the value of State from Needs Review to Translated or Final. If you need an approval process for the translation, you may need to use both Translated and Final.

You don't need to change the State value at all to use the translated text. These fields are included to help you manage your development workflow, but have no impact on how the files are compiled into resources.

If you used machine translation and want to correct or otherwise change the translated text, you can make your edits here. Once the value of State has been changed to Translated or Final, the MAT skips over that string the next time that machine translation is used.

If you make any changes to a string resource with the Multilingual Editor, remember to press Save in the command ribbon. Once you make a change, the Save button is enabled. If you forget to press it, the editor prompts you to save your changes when you close the editor.

Next, build the project to generate the .resx files. The MainPageText.es.resx and MainPageText.zh-Hans.resx files will be created if they do not yet exist or replaced if they do exist.

Now that you have the resources, it's time to use them in the code. First, you can create an interface in the shared code for changing the language. This interface defines the signature of the method that is called to change the language. The actual code to change the language is defined in each platform project file. In the project for the portable library, add a new class and name it ICultureOverride. Then replace all the existing code with the following:

```
namespace HelloWorld
{
    public interface ICultureOverride
    {
        void SetCultureOverride(string culture);
    }
}
```

You are defining a single method named SetCultureOverride() that takes a locale as a string parameter. Now that the interface is defined in the PCL, you need to define the implementation in the platform projects. The Android and iOS classes are essentially identical; the UWP project uses slightly different code. By implementing an interface, you hide the platform-specific implementations from the portable code.

In the Android project, add the CultureOverride class. Replace the default code with the following:

```
using System.Globalization;
using System.Threading;

namespace HelloWorld.Droid
{
    public class CultureOverride : ICultureOverride
    {
        public void SetCultureOverride(string culture)
        {
            Thread.CurrentThread.CurrentCulture = new CultureInfo(culture);
            Thread.CurrentThread.CurrentUICulture = Thread.CurrentThread.CurrentCulture;
        }
    }
}
```

The code is fairly simple. You are defining a new class and it will implement the ICultureOverride interface. This means it needs to provide a definition for the SetCultureOverride method. This method has just two lines. The following line sets the user locale (i.e., language and country) to the specified locale string. It controls date/time, number, and currency formatting:

```
Thread.CurrentThread.CurrentCulture = new CultureInfo(culture);
```

The second line sets the language used by the UI:

```
Thread.CurrentThread.CurrentUICulture = Thread.CurrentThread.CurrentCulture;
```

For Xamarin.Forms to use the platform code for the interface, you need to register the class via a metadata attribute. This registration allows the Xamarin.Forms DependencyService to locate the implantation class runtime. Above the name space definition, add the following line:

```
[assembly: Xamarin.Forms.Dependency(typeof(CultureOverride))]
```

Because the assembly attribute is referencing a class that is defined with a nondefault namespace, that namespace has to be added to the using list. Your class should now look like this:

```
using System.Globalization;
using System.Threading;
using HelloWorld.Droid;

[assembly: Xamarin.Forms.Dependency(typeof(CultureOverride))]
namespace HelloWorld.Droid
{
    public class CultureOverride : ICultureOverride
    {
        public void SetCultureOverride(string culture)
        {
            Thread.CurrentThread.CurrentCulture = new CultureInfo(culture);
            Thread.CurrentThread.CurrentUICulture = Thread.CurrentThread.CurrentCulture;
        }
    }
}
```

For iOS, follow the same steps. The only difference is in the addition of the nondefault namespace. You end up with the following:

```
using System.Globalization;
using System.Threading;
using HelloWorld.iOS;

[assembly: Xamarin.Forms.Dependency(typeof(CultureOverride))]
namespace HelloWorld.iOS
{
    public class CultureOverride : ICultureOverride
    {
        public void SetCultureOverride(string culture)
        {
```

```
        Thread.CurrentThread.CurrentCulture = new CultureInfo(culture);
        Thread.CurrentThread.CurrentUICulture = Thread.CurrentThread.CurrentCulture;
    }
  }
}
```

For the UWP app, the syntax is slightly different. Instead of setting `CurrentUICulture`, you set `ApplicationLanguages.PrimaryLanguageOverride`. So the UWP version of `CultureOverride.cs` looks like this:

```
using Windows.ApplicationModel.Resources.Core;
using HelloWorld.UWP;

[assembly: Xamarin.Forms.Dependency(typeof(CultureOverride))]
namespace HelloWorld.UWP
{
    public class CultureOverride : ICultureOverride
    {
        public void SetCultureOverride(string culture)
        {
            Windows.Globalization.ApplicationLanguages.PrimaryLanguageOverride = culture;
            ResourceContext.GetForCurrentView().Reset();
        }
    }
}
```

This definition of the CultureOverride class also behaves differently; `PrimaryLanguageOverride` is a "sticky" setting. If you change the language to Chinese and then restart the app, the app comes up Chinese as the default language. If you are using code to change the language for testing, you have need to remember that. To avoid that behavior, set `PrimaryLanguageOverride` to `string.Empty` in your startup code.

Now that you have language change implementation code, you have to add code to use the string resource and to wire up the buttons to code that will change the language.

In the code-behind file for the XAML page, add the following method:

```
private void UpdateText()
{
    LabelWelcome.Text = resources.MainPageText.Welcome;
}
```

This method updates the `Text` property to the string resource named Welcome. By default, the string resource file named `MainPageText.resx` provides the value of the string resource named `Welcome`. The .NET Framework tries to match the `CurrentUICulture` to the right resource file. If the language is set to Spanish, it tries to load the values from `MainPageText.es.resx`. If it can't find that file, the default of `MainPageText.resx` is used.

When you specify both the language and the culture with the locale string, the .NET Framework tries to find a match based on language and culture. If a match is not found, it tries to match by just the language. If that match fails, the default resource file is used. This search is done for each of the individual string resources, not the entire resource file.

Now add the method used to change the language and refresh the display:

```
private void ChangeCulture(string culture)
{
    DependencyService.Get<ICultureOverride>().SetCultureOverride(culture);
    UpdateText();
}
```

The Xamarin.Forms DependencyService finds the platform implementation for ICultureOverride and then calls the SetCultureOverride() method while passing in the locale. It then calls UpdateText() to refresh the display.

The final step is to wire up the button click event handlers to call the ChangeCulture() method:

```
public MainPage()
{
    InitializeComponent();

    BtnEnglish.Clicked += (sender, args) => { ChangeCulture("en"); };
    BtnSpanish.Clicked += (sender, args) => { ChangeCulture("es"); };
    BtnChinese.Clicked += (sender, args) => { ChangeCulture("zh-Hans"); };

    UpdateText();
}
```

For each button press, ChangeCulture() is called with the appropriate language passed in.

For more elaborate Xamarin.Forms apps, you can leverage the MVVM functionality that is provided with Xamarin.Forms and put more of the code in the XAML.

░ **Note** MVVM, which stands for Model-View-ViewModel, is a software architecture pattern that separates the data and business logic from the UI code. (MVVM is covered in greater detail in Chapter 4.)

You should be able to compile and run the app. The next chapter builds an entire app with source that can be downloaded.

When you run on Android, you should see a screen that looks like Figure 3-12.

Figure 3-12. *Sample app using the default language*

Clicking the Spanish button changes the display to look like Figure 3-13.

Figure 3-13. *Sample app using Spanish*

And clicking the Chinese button shows the display shown in Figure 3-14.

Figure 3-14. *Sample app using Chinese (Simplified)*

If you had not added the language change buttons, you could get the same results by changing the language in the settings app for the device.

These screenshots were taken from the Visual Studio Emulator for Android. When testing localization on an app, you should use an emulated device. If you change the language and can't figure out how to change it back to the previous one, it's much easier to reset an emulator than an actual device.

CHAPTER 4

Island Menu Application

I know all those words, but that sentence makes no sense to me.

—Matt Groening

To demonstrate the process of localizing an application, in this chapter you'll build one from scratch by using Xamarin.Forms and target Android, iOS, and UWP. You'll start with just a single language, English, which will be written to support multiple languages. You'll then add some additional languages. The last step is to add some platform-specific code to display the app name in the translated language on the app launcher screens.

About the App

The application is called Island Menu (named for the tourist board of the island of St. Brian, which is a Mediterranean island that is a popular tourist destination). With its deep harbor, cruise ships make daily stops there.

The tourist board will arrange to have the app available for guests on the cruise ships. The tourists then have the opportunity to see what restaurants are on the island.

Note You can't find a Wikipedia page for the island of St. Brian; it exists only for the purpose of doing this application. But it looks like a nice place to visit.

The app will display a list of St. Brian restaurants, with locations and phone numbers. When users tap on a restaurant, they will see a page for that restaurant with a list of menu items; and each menu item will show the name of the dish, a description of that dish, and the price in euros.

When the localization is completed for the application, the labels will be translated to the current language. Date and number formatting will be set to the current culture. The menu data will be localized with the menu item name and description in the current language.

A completed version of the app can be downloaded from [INSERT SOURCE CODE URL HERE]. You should have a copy of it to use as a source for the images and data files.

© Christopher Miller 2017
C. Miller, *Cross-platform Localization for Native Mobile Apps with Xamarin*,
DOI 10.1007/978-1-4842-2466-3_4

App Architecture

You use Xamarin.Forms to build the Island Menu app, so you can share about 99% of the code. The remaining platform-specific code is for the localization of the app name.

One of the benefits of using Xamarin.Forms is that the MVVM display pattern is included right out of the box. Using MVVM, which stands for Model-View-View-Model, is a popular way of separating the UI code from the business logic.

At a high level, the model represents your data structure, which can be the data that comes from your database or some internal structure. It can represent the actual data or it can be part of the data access layer.

The *view* is the code that defines what appears onscreen. It handles the controls, layout, and some of the behavior. With Xamarin.Forms, the view can be constructed using XAML or in code. The sample app that you will build in this chapter uses XAML.

The view model abstracts the view to a set of properties and commands. It "binds" the data from the model to the view and maintains the state of the data. The view model has the code (or calls the code) that handles the saving and loading of data.

By using MVVM, you can take advantage of the data binding that comes with XAML and eliminate nearly all the code to send data to the screen and pull it back from the screen. You will use the declarative binding that comes with the Xamarin XAML to wire up properties exposed in the view model.

One thing that you don't get automatically with data binding is the translation of the text strings in the resource files. Although you could handle it by populating the controls at runtime with code, there is another way. XAML allows you to create converters to transform your code. You will add a converter that will use your resource files to get the translated data to populate the view.

Supplying Data to the App

With this type of app, you have a couple of choices for determining where the data comes from. Most of the time, it is pulled from a web service of some sort. Sometimes it may just be hard coded as part of the application. Most apps download the data to provide the most current information.

To keep this app simple for testing, you'll use a set of embedded data, but the app will be built as if it were getting the data from a web service. For the purposes of this example application, you don't need a full web back end; the static data is enough.

Building the Island Menu App

You can start by creating a new application. The app created for this book was done with Visual Studio 2015 running on Windows 10. If you are using different versions, some of the options may have different names or be unavailable. Development of Windows 10 UWP apps requires you to be running on Windows 10.

It's also assumed that you have Xamarin and the Multilingual App Toolkit (MAT) installed. And it's also assumed that you have the current Android SDK installed if you are doing the Android project. The version of Xamarin.Forms used for this book is 2.3.

To do iOS development with Xamarin, you have to have a Mac available with the Xamarin tools already installed. You can do all the coding and debugging from Visual Studio, but it uses the Mac to compile and run the iOS code. If a Mac is not available, you can follow along and do the Android and Windows 10 UWP apps.

▓ **Note** Although a Mac is needed to compile and debug the iOS project, you don't need an expensive Mac. As long as the Mac can run the current version of MacOS (what was formerly known as OS X), you should be set.

Start up Visual Studio and create a new project. Select the Blank Xaml App (Xamarin.Forms Portable) template. The sample project named the app IslandMenu. You can name it anything you want, but the namespaces used by the app are based on IslandMenu.

Visual Studio churns for a bit and generates a solution with multiple projects. For this sample application, you are doing only the Android, iOS, and Windows UWP projects. You should delete the Windows 8 and Windows Phone 8 projects from the solution. Although you can use them, stick to UWP for the Windows version of the app to keep things simple.

Now that the solution and projects are in place, you need to restore and update the nuget packages. Right-click the solution and select Manage Nuget Packages. If the Xamarin.Forms package needs to be updated, select it and press Update.

You may need to fill in a license dialog or accept additional package updates to get the current version of Xamarin.Forms. The PCL project and each platform project should be updated.

You need to add one more library: Newtonsoft.Json, which is the de facto standard on .NET for working with JSON files. While the nuget package manager is still loaded, click the online tab and type **newtonsoft** into the search tab. Select the Newtonsoft.Json package and press Install. This package is needed only for the PCL project.

Once the nuget packages are updated, it is a good time to compile the solution and make sure that all the components are in place. You should be able to compile and run each platform. The default template for a Xamarin.Forms app is the Xamarin.Forms version of "Hello World".

If you can't run the default template, you have to address the problem before continuing. The Xamarin supplied templates should work out of the box.

Create the Folders

Now that you have a working project, you can create some folders in the shared code project. Although not required, organizing the project into folders can make it easier to follow the code.

Right-click IslandMenu project and select Add and then Folder. Name the folder **Models**. The Models folder will contain the models for the restaurants and their menu items. You will come back and start with the models after creating the rest of the folders. Create the following folders:

1. Add a folder named **Views**. This folder will have the restaurant list view and the menu list views.

2. Add a folder named **ViewModels**. In this folder you will create the view model used by both views.

3. Add a folder named **Services**. The code that does the data access will be in this folder. Because this app is emulating a web service by loading static files, these files will be in the folder as well.

4. The **Resources** folder is the next folder to add. The `.resx` resource files will be in this folder, along with some helper classes. You could put the helper classes in another folder, but this should be sufficient.

5. The last folder to add is a folder named **Images**. You will bundle some images to use with each restaurant. If you pulled your data from a web service, you could send back URLs for each image. With this project, the images will be bundled in with the app. You can copy the images from the completed project file or substitute your own.

When you bundle images in with an app, you usually place the apps in the graphics folders for each platform, which allows you to use different-sized images for different resolutions. iOS has standard size, 2x Retina, and 3x Retina. Android has standard DPI, Medium DPI, High DPI, Extra High DPI, and extra.

This app takes a much simpler route to bundling the images. Instead of having multiple sets of images for the platform, there will be just a single set of images. You will add a custom IValueConverter that will take the name of the image and load it from the resource assembly.

Define the Models

Now it's time to define the models for your data. When the app is running, there will be a list of restaurants, each showing a list of menus.

One way of defining models is from the bottom up. Start with the simplest model and work up to the more complex models, which means starting with the menu items. Define a model class for the menu items and name it **RestaurantMenuItem**, as described here.

░ **Note**   The class is deliberately named RestaurantMenuItem instead of MenuItem because there are too many UI classes out there named MenuItem. Giving your model the same name as a UI element opens the door to all sorts of namespace complications. It would work, but it would take more code.

Right-click the Models folder and select Add and then Class. Name the class **RestaurantMenuItem**. This process creates the class RestaurantMenuItem.cs with the bare template of a class definition. Use the following for the class definition:

```
namespace IslandMenu.Models
{
    public class RestaurantMenuItem
    {
        public string Name { get; set; }
        public string Language { get; set; }
        public string Description { get; set; }
        public decimal PriceInEuros { get; set; }
    }
}
```

If you used a different namespace for your project, use your names. The field definitions are mostly self-descriptive, as shown in Table 4-1.

Table 4-1. *Definitions of the RestaurantMenuItem Properties*

Field Name	Description
Name	Name of the menu item
Language	Locale code for this translation
Description	Description of what the menu item is
PriceInEuros	Local price of the item in euros (€)

░ **Note** This demo doesn't handle currency conversion. If you want do so, you can find a web service that provides the level service to match your needs. There are free services, but their usage usually has fixed limits. Chapter 5 has more information about using currency exchange services.

Now that you have the menu item definition, it's time to create the Restaurant class. Right-click the Models folder and add a new class named **Restaurant**. As with the menu item, a new file named Restaurant.cs is added. Replace the default class definition with the following, taking care to respect your own namespace rules:

```
namespace IslandMenu.Models
{
    public class Restaurant
    {
        public int ID { get; set; }
        public string Name { get; set; }
        public string Address1 { get; set; }
        public string Address2 { get; set; }
        public string Town { get; set; }
        public string PhoneNumber { get; set; }
        public string Fax { get; set; }
        public string Photo { get; set; }
        public List<RestaurantMenuItem> Menu { get; set; }
    }
}
```

The field definitions map to the functionality that is needed in the app. Definitions of the properties are shown in Table 4-2.

Table 4-2. *Definitions of the Restaurant Class Properties*

Field Name	Description
ID	Placeholder for a record ID (not used here)
Name	Name of the restaurant
Address1	Street address
Address2	Additional address information (not used here)
Town	Name of the town
PhoneNumber	Phone number with full country code
Fax	Fax number (not used here)
Photo	File name or URL of the photo
Menu	Collection of menu items for the restaurant

Each restaurant has just one language translation loaded at a time. Because the user will be changing the language from within the app, you can just load the set for the current language.

▓ **Note** Why not create a restaurants list or a menu list class in your Models folder? The goal is to use a model to define what an entity is and keep the definitions simple. Collections of entities are what the view model classes manage.

Services Layer

Now that the data models are defined, it's time to write the code to retrieve the data. If you were calling a web service to get the data, the data would probably come back in JSON or XML format. This app uses static JSON files that are embedded resources and passes them back as if they were called from a web service.

The first files added to the Services folder are data files. (Because the data is too long to put in this book, you can take them from the sample code posted here: [INSERT CODE URL HERE]). The data.json file is the default language version and is what you get if you have an object that is a List<Restaurant> and serialized as JSON. A brief portion of that JSON file looks like this:

```
[
  {
    "ID": 1,
    "Name": "First Chance Pizza",
    "Address1": "421 Cami de Sant Esteban",
    "Address2": null,
    "Town": "Carlyle",
    "PhoneNumber": "+70 971 24 13 55",
    "Fax": "+70 971 24 13 58",
    "Photo": "firstchancepizza.jpg",
    "Menu": [
      {
        "Name": "Classic Pizza",
        "CategoryId": 1,
        "Language": null,
        "Description": "Classic pizza, the way you get it in the USA",
        "PriceInEuros": 6.1
      },
      {
        "Name": "First Chance Pizza",
        "CategoryId": 1,
        "Language": null,
        "Description": "Our signature pizza, made with all local ingredients",
        "PriceInEuros": 12.20
      }
    ]
  },
  {
    "ID": 2,
    "Name": "Club Continental",
    "Address1": "Av. del Port de Sant Brian",
    "Address2": null,
```

```
"Town": "Port de St Brian",
"PhoneNumber": "+70 971 32 16 70",
"Fax": null,
"Photo": "clubcontinental.jpg",
"Menu": [
  {
    "Name": "Club Continental",
    "CategoryId": 1,
    "Language": null,
    "Description": "Our signature sandwich.  The classic club, done perfectly",
    "PriceInEuros": 8.0
  },
...
```

This is an abbreviated set of data and does not have the closing JSON tags. The finished project has full versions of the `.json` files. For multiple languages, there are files that use the locale as part of the name, which is the same file-naming format used by the resource files. For example, the Spanish versions are named `data-es.json` or `data-es-ES.json`.

■ **Note**   You should have been able to name the data file `data.es.json`, and the .NET resource manager would have loaded the correct file at runtime based on the current locale value. This did not work correctly, so you'll add some code to load the correct file.

Make sure to set the `Build Action` property to `EmbeddedResource` for each of the JSON files. This setting is needed to be able to access them at runtime.

■ **Note**   If you add a file as a resource and it doesn't show up at runtime, check the `Build Action` property. If it's not set to `EmbeddedResource`, it will still compile, but it just won't work.

Using the DependencyService

To pass the current locale to the service code, you have to get the current value. This code is platform specific and requires library methods not accessible from a PCL.

You can use a Xamarin.Forms implementation of dependency injection to provide access in the PCL to the user's locale (language and country) setting that is defined and set in the platform (Android, iOS, UWP) projects. The DependencyService in Xamarin.Forms allows you to define an interface in the shared code and then load the platform-specific implementation at runtime.

There are three sets of code that you need to build to use the DependencyService. Follow these steps:

1.   Add an interface in the shared code to provide a definition of the fields to be used in the PCL code.

2.   Add the platform-specific implementations and register them. This is where the fields that were defined in the interface get populated.

3.   In the shared code, make an explicit call to the DependencyService and ask it for an implementation of that interface.

Defining the Interface

Right-click the IslandMenu project; add a new class and name it **ICultureInfo.cs**. This class defines the properties to be set in the platform-specific code. Replace the default code with the following:

```
namespace IslandMenu
{
    public interface ICultureInfo
    {
        System.Globalization.CultureInfo CurrentCulture { get; set; }
        System.Globalization.CultureInfo CurrentUICulture { get; set; }
    }
}
```

There's not much to it; the interface is just defining the CurrentCulture and CurrentUICulture properties. Now that the interface is defined, it is time to add the platform implementations.

Platform Implementations

Start with the Android project, IslandMenu.Droid. Right-click that project; add a new class and name it **PlatformCultureInfo.cs**. Replace the default code with the following:

```
using Xamarin.Forms;
using System.Threading;

[assembly: Dependency(typeof(IslandMenu.Droid.PlatformCultureInfo))]
namespace IslandMenu.Droid
{
    class PlatformCultureInfo : ICultureInfo
    {
        public System.Globalization.CultureInfo CurrentCulture
        {
            get
            {
                return Thread.CurrentThread.CurrentCulture;
            }
            set
            {
                Thread.CurrentThread.CurrentCulture = value;
            }
        }

        public System.Globalization.CultureInfo CurrentUICulture
        {
            get
            {
                return Thread.CurrentThread.CurrentUICulture;
            }
            set
            {
```

```
                Thread.CurrentThread.CurrentUICulture = value;
            }
        }
    }
}
```

This code provides the implementation of the ICultureInfo interface. It gets and sets the properties by using the Thread.CurrentThread object. This object is not available to use from the PCL, which is why it needs to be referenced from the implementation code at the platform project.

The Dependency attribute right above the namespace declaration registers this implementation. This registration allows the DependencyService to find this implementation at runtime.

Now you need to do the same thing for iOS. Add a new class to the IslandMenu.iOS project and also name it **PlatformCultureInfo.cs**. Use the following code:

```
using Xamarin.Forms;
using System.Threading;

[assembly: Dependency(typeof(IslandMenu.iOS.PlatformCultureInfo))]
namespace IslandMenu.iOS
{
    class PlatformCultureInfo : ICultureInfo
    {
        public System.Globalization.CultureInfo CurrentCulture
        {
            get
            {
                return Thread.CurrentThread.CurrentCulture;
            }
            set
            {
                Thread.CurrentThread.CurrentCulture = value;
            }
        }

        public System.Globalization.CultureInfo CurrentUICulture
        {
            get
            {
                return Thread.CurrentThread.CurrentUICulture;
            }
            set
            {
                Thread.CurrentThread.CurrentUICulture = value;
            }
        }
    }
}
```

As you can see, the only difference between the Android and the iOS code is the namespace. The code in the Windows 10 UWP project is a little different, however.

With the IslandMenu.UWP project, add the `PlatformCultureInfo.cs` class. Now replace the code with the following:

```
using System.Globalization;
using Xamarin.Forms;

[assembly: Dependency(typeof(IslandMenu.UWP.PlatformCultureInfo))]
namespace IslandMenu.UWP
{
    class PlatformCultureInfo : ICultureInfo
    {
        public System.Globalization.CultureInfo CurrentCulture
        {
            get
            {
                return CultureInfo.CurrentCulture;
            }
            set
            {
                CultureInfo.CurrentCulture = value;
            }
        }

        public System.Globalization.CultureInfo CurrentUICulture
        {
            get
            {
                return CultureInfo.CurrentUICulture;
            }
            set
            {
                CultureInfo.CurrentUICulture = value;
            }
        }
    }
}
```

The code is similar, but it uses the `System.Globalization.CultureInfo` object instead of the `Thread.CurrentThread` object. The remaining piece of using the `DependencyService` will be added when the view model is defined later on.

Data Access

Now it's time to add the code to retrieve the data. In the Services folder, add a new class and name it **DataServices**. Replace the default class definition with the following code:

```
using System.Collections.Generic;
using System.IO;
using System.Reflection;
using System.Threading.Tasks;
```

```
using IslandMenu.Models;
using Newtonsoft.Json;

namespace IslandMenu.Services
{
    public class DataServices
    {
        public async Task<IEnumerable<Restaurant>> GetRestaurants(string locale)
        {
            var language = GetClosestLanguage(locale);
            var assembly = typeof(DataServices).GetTypeInfo().Assembly;
            var json = "";

            var stream = assembly.GetManifestResourceStream($"IslandMenu.Services.
                        data{language}.json") ??
                    assembly.GetManifestResourceStream("IslandMenu.Services.data.json");

            using (var reader = new StreamReader(stream))
            {
                json = await reader.ReadToEndAsync();
            }

            var restaurants = JsonConvert.DeserializeObject<List<Restaurant>>(json);

            return restaurants;
        }

        private static string GetClosestLanguage(string locale)
        {
            var langs = new[]{ "es", "de", "zh" };
            var result = "";

            foreach(var lang in langs)
            {
                if (locale.StartsWith(lang))
                {
                    result = $"-{lang}";
                    break;
                }
            }

            return result;
        }
    }
}
```

You are defining two methods, one public and the other private. The GetClosestLanguage() method takes the locale string as the sole parameter. The method defines an internal string array called langs, which is a list of the supported locales for the data files.

> **Note** In this example, the code that determines which language file to use is just an artifact of mocking up the web service with a local data call. A real-world application could just send the current locale to the web service and let the web service decide which language to support.

The method iterates over the langs array and checks to see whether any supported locale matches the passed-in locale string. With the StartsWith() method, the code matches by the closest matching item. If you get a match, prefix that match with a "-" and return that match. Otherwise, return an empty string. That empty string forces the selection of the default data file.

The real action is in the GetRestaurants() method. It's defined as an async method and returns a Task<<IEnumerable<Restaurant>>. When writing code that consumes web services, you want to should use the async and await design patterns as much as possible. The last thing that you want is for your UI to freeze while data is being retrieved.

For a method that is reading from an embedded resource, the data access is fast enough that async calls are not really needed. One of the advantages of using the .NET Framework is the deep support using async methods. Even if the code doesn't really need it, it's good practice to follow the asynch design patterns.

Review the rest of the method line by line:

```
var language = GetClosestLanguage(locale);
```

As discussed previously, try to find the closest match for the specified locale:

```
var assembly = typeof(DataServices).GetTypeInfo().Assembly;
```

Using reflection, get a reference to the Assembly that has the data files as an embedded resource:

```
var stream = assembly.GetManifestResourceStream($"IslandMenu.Services.data{language}.json") ??
            assembly.GetManifestResourceStream("IslandMenu.Services.data.json");
```

Open the specified JSON file as a stream. Use the null-coalescing operator "??" to try loading the localized file. If it doesn't exist, the GetManifestResourceStream() method returns null. If that happens, load the default data file:

```
using (var reader = new StreamReader(stream))
{
    json = await reader.ReadToEndAsync();
}
```

Using the async method for reading, you can read the entire JSON file in as a string:

```
var restaurants = JsonConvert.DeserializeObject<List<Restaurant>>(json);

return restaurants;
```

With the JSON data in a string variable, use the Newtonsoft deserializer to load up a new list of restaurants and return that list to the calling method.

If you were calling a web service method, the same async pattern could be used like this:

```
static async Task<IEnumerable<Restaurant>> GetRestaurantsAsync(string path)
{
    List<Restaurant> restaurants = null;
    HttpResponseMessage response = await client.GetAsync(path);
    if (response.IsSuccessStatusCode)
    {
        restaurants = await response.Content.ReadAsAsync<List<Restaurant>>();
    }
    return restaurants;
}
```

From the view model, a call to get the data looks the same for both the static data and the web service call.

Note One of the benefits of using the MVVM pattern is that you can test your data models and data access code completely separately from the UI code. The models are pure POCO (Plain Old Clr Objects, which are classes that have no other framework dependencies), and the data access code for web services is usually portable across various .NET implementations.

View Model

With the data model and the data access code defined, you can add a view model to the project. In the ViewModels folder, add a class named **RestaurantsViewModel**. As you did with the other classes, replace the default code with the following:

```
using System;
using System.Collections.Generic;
using System.Threading.Tasks;
using IslandMenu.Models;
using IslandMenu.Services;
using Xamarin.Forms;

namespace IslandMenu.ViewModels
{
    public class RestaurantsViewModel
    {
        public string ImageUrl { get; private set; }
        public string LastUpdate { get; private set; }
        public IEnumerable<Restaurant> Restaurants { get; private set; }

        public INavigation Navigation { get; set; }

        public RestaurantsViewModel()
        {
            ImageUrl = "islandmenubanner.jpg";
            Restaurants = GetRestaurants().Result;
        }
    }
```

```
        private async Task<IEnumerable<Restaurant>> GetRestaurants()
        {
            var ds = new DataServices();
            LastUpdate = String.Format(Resources.IslandMenu.LastUpdate, DateTime.Now.ToString("D"));
            var cultureInfo = Xamarin.Forms.DependencyService.Get<ICultureInfo>();

            return await ds.GetRestaurants(cultureInfo.CurrentCulture.Name);          }
    }
}
```

You are defining some properties and some code to populate the properties. When the view model is assigned to the view through the BindingContext property, the visual controls can be bound to those properties.

The ImageUrl property is used to display a background image on the main page. LastUpdate displays the date of the data access. Restaurants is the list that gets bound to the list in the view. The Navigation property allows the app to pass navigation control from the main page so that the menu page launches when the user taps the restaurant from the list.

The GetRestaurants() method is used to populate the data and is called from the view model's constructor. More elaborate apps could wire up buttons to call this method to refresh the list. This implementation news up an instance of the data service and updates the LastUpdate property using the current date and a string resource as the template for string formatting. Although most of the string translation is in the view, it can be easier to work with parameterized strings in the view mode code.

The final part of the DependencyService is used in the GetRestaurants() method. Calling DependencyService.Get<ICultureInfo>() returns an instance of the platform implementation of the ICultureInfo interface.

XAML Markup Extensions

Now that you have the view model, you need to add two XAML markup extensions. One is an extension that lets you use localized text in the declarative XAML markup code. The other is a converter lets you load the images from the shared code resource file.

ImageResourceConverter

In the Resources folder, add a class named **ImageResourceConverter**. As usual, replace the default class definition with the following:

```
using System;
using Xamarin.Forms;

namespace IslandMenu.Resources
{
    public class ImageResourceConverter : IValueConverter
    {
        public object Convert(object value, Type targetType, object parameter, System.
Globalization.CultureInfo culture)
        {
            return ImageSource.FromResource("IslandMenu.Images." + (value ?? ""));
        }
```

```
        public object ConvertBack(object value, Type targetType, object parameter, System.
Globalization.CultureInfo culture)
        {
            throw new NotSupportedException();
        }
    }
}
```

An IValueConverter is a filter that takes a value and returns an interpreted version of that value. It can go in both directions: from the view model to the view and from the view back to the view model. The latter uses a method named ConvertBack(). Because this app is not doing two-way data binding on the images, you don't need to do anything with the ConvertBack() method; it throws an exception if it's called.

The method that you do care about is the Convert() method:

```
public object Convert(object value, Type targetType, object parameter, System.Globalization.
CultureInfo culture)
{
    return ImageSource.FromResource("IslandMenu.Images." + (value ?? ""));
}
```

It takes the passed-in value (the name of the image file) and constructs a fully qualified name with the namespace for the folder that has the images. With the full name, the code uses the ImageSource. FromResource() method and returns an instance of ImageSource from the embedded resource. The ImageSource class is part of Xamarin.Forms and is used to load images from files or URLs. With this IValueConverter, you can bind images from the embedded resources to visual controls in the view.

TranslateExtension

The second XAML extension handles the resource file lookup of the translated strings. Add another class to the Resources folder and name it **TranslateExtension**. Once more, replace the default class definition with the following code:

```
using System;
using Xamarin.Forms;
using Xamarin.Forms.Xaml;

namespace IslandMenu.Resources
{
    // Define the default content property
    [ContentProperty("Text")]
    public class TranslateExtension : IMarkupExtension
    {
        public string Text { get; set; }

        public object ProvideValue(IServiceProvider serviceProvider)
        {
            if (Text == null)
                return null;
```

```
            // Return the localized resource if available, default resource if not
            return IslandMenu.ResourceManager.GetString(Text, IslandMenu.Culture);
        }
    }
}
```

▓ **Note**   This is an `IMarkupExtension` implementation, based on code originally posted by Craig Dunn at Microsoft. To see the original forum post, in which Craig describes his implementation, please see https://forums.xamarin.com/discussion/comment/82834/#Comment_82834.

An IMarkupExtension lets you extend XAML by adding new properties or functionality. In this case, you are adding a Translate verb to XAML. It defines the Text property as the content property, which means that whatever property that is passed the Translate extension, you can reference its value through the Text property. In the ProvideValue() method, you take the Text property (assuming that it's not null) and call the GetString() method ResourceManager property of the IslandMenu resource. GetString()returns a localized value for that Text value if it exists. If a localized value is not defined, the default value is used.

Adding the Views

The next step is to add the XAML that makes up the views. To initially create the views, the author used a tool named Gorilla Player from UXDivers, which is an XAML preview tool that lets you view the XAML on a device or emulator as you type. Using Gorilla Player is not a requirement to be able to write the XAML code, but it provides a way to preview the code at design time.

Define Some Style

A benefit of using Gorilla Player is that it provides some nice sample code for styling the XAML. You will use one of the styles to quickly add a modern look to the app.

Open the App.xaml file, which is in the root folder of the portable library. The default template for the App.xaml file looks something like this:

```
<?xml version="1.0" encoding="utf-8" ?>
<Application xmlns="http://xamarin.com/schemas/2014/forms"
             xmlns:x="http://schemas.microsoft.com/winfx/2009/xaml"
             x:Class="IslandMenu.App">
  <Application.Resources>

    <!-- Application resource dictionary -->

  </Application.Resources>
</Application>
```

Replace the line that contains Application resource dictionary with the following XAML markup:

```
<ResourceDictionary>
  <Color x:Key="CardBackgroundColor">#AA000000</Color>
  <Color x:Key="MessageBoxBackgroundColor">#99212331</Color>
  <Color x:Key="TitleBoxBackgroundColor">#99FFFFFF</Color>
  <Color x:Key="NameColor">#ffffff</Color>
```

```xml
<Color x:Key="DepartmentColor">#b0bec5</Color>
<Color x:Key="LocationColor">#40c4ff</Color>
<Color x:Key="MoreIconColor">#1de9b6</Color>
<Color x:Key="SocialColor">#40c4ff</Color>
<Color x:Key="MessageColor">White</Color>
<Color x:Key="TitleBoxTextColor">Black</Color>
<Color x:Key="EntryBackgroundColor">#7778909c</Color>

<Style x:Key="CardStyle" TargetType="Grid">
  <Setter Property="HeightRequest" Value="80"/>
  <Setter Property="Padding" Value="5,10,0,10"/>
  <Setter Property="BackgroundColor" Value="{DynamicResource CardBackgroundColor}"/>
</Style>

<Style x:Key="MessageBox" TargetType="Grid">
  <Setter Property="HeightRequest" Value="25"/>
  <Setter Property="Padding" Value="10"/>
  <Setter Property="BackgroundColor" Value="{DynamicResource MessageBoxBackgroundColor}"/>
</Style>

<Style x:Key="TitleBox" TargetType="Grid">
  <Setter Property="HeightRequest" Value="25"/>
  <Setter Property="Padding" Value="10"/>
  <Setter Property="BackgroundColor" Value="{DynamicResource TitleBoxBackgroundColor}"/>
</Style>

<Style x:Key="TitleStyle" TargetType="Label">
  <Setter Property="FontSize" Value="20"/>
  <Setter Property="TextColor" Value="{DynamicResource TitleBoxTextColor}"/>
  <Setter Property="FontAttributes" Value="Bold"/>
</Style>

<Style x:Key="TitleStyleSmall" TargetType="Label">
  <Setter Property="FontSize" Value="16"/>
  <Setter Property="TextColor" Value="{DynamicResource TitleBoxTextColor}"/>
</Style>

<Style x:Key="ShadowStyle" TargetType="BoxView">
  <Setter Property="HeightRequest" Value="1"/>
  <Setter Property="BackgroundColor" Value="Black"/>
</Style>

<Style x:Key="NameStyle" TargetType="Label">
  <Setter Property="FontSize" Value="16"/>
  <Setter Property="TextColor" Value="{DynamicResource NameColor}"/>
  <Setter Property="FontAttributes" Value="Bold"/>
</Style>

<Style x:Key="DepartmentStyle" TargetType="Label">
  <Setter Property="FontSize" Value="14"/>
  <Setter Property="TextColor" Value="{DynamicResource DepartmentColor}"/>
</Style>
```

65

```xml
<Style x:Key="LocationStyle" TargetType="Label">
  <Setter Property="FontSize" Value="9"/>
  <Setter Property="TextColor" Value="{DynamicResource LocationColor}"/>
  <Setter Property="FontAttributes" Value="Bold"/>
</Style>

<Style x:Key="MoreStyle" TargetType="Label">
  <Setter Property="FontSize" Value="10"/>
  <Setter Property="TextColor" Value="{DynamicResource MoreIconColor}"/>
  <Setter Property="FontAttributes" Value="Bold"/>
  <Setter Property="HorizontalTextAlignment" Value="End"/>
</Style>

<Style x:Key="SocialStyle" TargetType="Label">
  <Setter Property="FontSize" Value="10"/>
  <Setter Property="TextColor" Value="{DynamicResource SocialColor}"/>
</Style>

<Style x:Key="MessageLabelStyle" TargetType="Label">
  <Setter Property="TextColor" Value="{DynamicResource MessageColor}"/>
  <Setter Property="FontSize" Value="8"/>
  <Setter Property="VerticalOptions" Value="Center"/>
  <Setter Property="FontAttributes" Value="Bold"/>
</Style>

<Style x:Key="MessageEntryStyle" TargetType="Label">
  <Setter Property="FontAttributes" Value="Bold"/>
</Style>
</ResourceDictionary>
```

This code defines some tags to set colors and other attributes in the XAML markup. Using styles defined at the application level makes it easier to make global changes to the styling of the application.

Using a Modular Design

You'll build the XAML in a modular fashion. There are two forms, the restaurant list and the menu list, and each uses the Xamarin.Forms ListView control.

The Xamarin.Forms ListView control provides a level of abstraction from the platform-specific UI toolkits. At runtime, the ListView control is rendered as the platform native control. On Android and Windows, the native ListView control is rendered. For iOS, the ListView control is rendered using the UITableView control.

With each ListView, ListItem is defined to display each item in the list. Although you could define the ListItem XAML inside the ListView XAML, for this project you define the ListItems as separate files. When you use design tools, it can be easier to work with the individual parts of a page.

RestaurantItem View

To define the restaurant item, right-click the Views folder; select Add and then New Item. From the left-side tree, select Cross-Platform under Visual C#. Then select Forms Xaml View, enter **RestaurantItem.xaml**, and click Add. An empty `ContentView` container is created. Replace the contents of the new view with the following (make sure to change the namespace if you did not use the IslandMenu name):

```
<?xml version="1.0" encoding="UTF-8"?>
<ContentView xmlns="http://xamarin.com/schemas/2014/forms"
             xmlns:x="http://schemas.microsoft.com/winfx/2009/xaml"
             xmlns:translate="clr-namespace:IslandMenu.Resources;assembly=IslandMenu"
             x:Class="IslandMenu.Views.RestaurantItem">
  <ContentPage.Resources>
    <ResourceDictionary>
      <translate:ImageResourceConverter x:Key="imageResourceCvt" />
    </ResourceDictionary>
  </ContentPage.Resources>
  <ContentView.Content>
    <StackLayout Spacing="0" Padding="0">
      <Grid Style="{DynamicResource CardStyle}">
        <Grid.ColumnDefinitions>
          <ColumnDefinition Width="90"/>
          <ColumnDefinition Width="*"/>
          <ColumnDefinition Width="5"/>
        </Grid.ColumnDefinitions>

        <Image Grid.Column="0" Source="{Binding Photo, Converter={StaticResource imageResourceCvt}}"/>
        <StackLayout Grid.Column="1" Spacing="0" Padding="0,5">
          <Label Text="{Binding Name}" Style="{DynamicResource NameStyle}"/>
          <Grid>
            <Grid.ColumnDefinitions>
              <ColumnDefinition Width="Auto"/>
              <ColumnDefinition Width="*"/>
            </Grid.ColumnDefinitions>
            <Grid.RowDefinitions>
              <RowDefinition Height="Auto"/>
              <RowDefinition Height="Auto"/>
            </Grid.RowDefinitions>
            <Label Text="{translate:Translate Address}" Style="{DynamicResource MessageLabelStyle}"
                Grid.Row="0" Grid.Column="0"/>
              <Label Text="{Binding Address1}" Style="{DynamicResource DepartmentStyle}"
                Grid.Row="0" Grid.Column="1"/>
              <Label Text="{translate:Translate Town}" Style="{DynamicResource MessageLabelStyle}"
                Grid.Row="1" Grid.Column="0"/>
              <Label Text="{Binding Town}" Style="{DynamicResource DepartmentStyle}"
                Grid.Row="1" Grid.Column="1"/>
          </Grid>
        </StackLayout>
      </Grid>

      <BoxView BackgroundColor="Black" HeightRequest="0.5"></BoxView>
```

```
    <Grid Style="{DynamicResource MessageBox}">
      <StackLayout Orientation="Horizontal">
        <Label Text="{translate:Translate Phone}" Style="{DynamicResource MessageLabelStyle}" />
        <Label Text="{Binding PhoneNumber}" HorizontalOptions="FillAndExpand"
               BackgroundColor="#33ffffff" ></Label>
      </StackLayout>
    </Grid>

    <BoxView Style="{DynamicResource ShadowStyle}"></BoxView>
  </StackLayout>

</ContentView.Content>
</ContentView>
```

There is a bunch of stuff going on, most of it dealing with defining the layout. There is also code to handle data binding and localization. Starting at the top, you see this line:

```
xmlns:translate="clr-namespace:IslandMenu.Resources;assembly=IslandMenu"
```

This code defines the namespace so that the custom converters can be referenced. Define an XAML key to let you call the IMarkupConverter to load images from the assembly:

```
<ContentPage.Resources>
  <ResourceDictionary>
    <translate:ImageResourceConverter x:Key="imageResourceCvt" />
  </ResourceDictionary>
</ContentPage.Resources>
```

This code defines a key named imageResourceCvt that can be used in the XAML markup. At runtime, it invokes the ImageResourceConverter class. This converter, which is used for the restaurant photo, is set up with this line:

```
<Image Grid.Column="0" Source="{Binding Photo, Converter={StaticResource
imageResourceCvt}}"/>
```

Using XAML data binding, the app gets the value of the Photo property and sends it through the ImageResourceConverter. The converter attempts to load the image from the assembly and pass the bitmap stream to the image control. What is not shown here is the way the BindingContext property of the image control is being set. The BindingContext property connects the owner of the Photo property of the image, which is set at runtime when the view model is instantiated.

The text controls are defined like the following XAML:

```
<Label Text="{translate:Translate Address}" Style="{DynamicResource MessageLabelStyle}"
Grid.Row="0" Grid.Column="0"/>
```

```
<Label Text="{Binding Address1}" Style="{DynamicResource DepartmentStyle}" Grid.Row="0"
Grid.Column="1"/>
```

The first Label control uses the TranslateExtension to take the Address property and look up the value from the resource files. The second label uses the regular data binding to assign the value of the Address1 property to the Label control.

▓ **Note** You probably noticed that the IMarkupExtension was defined with the class name TranslateExtension, but referenced it in the XAML markup as Translate. It is just a naming convention that goes back years to when extensions were first added to WPF.

RestaurantList view

Now that you have the restaurant item, it's time to create the restaurant list. Add a new view to the Views folder, but instead of using the Forms Xaml View template, select the Forms Xaml Page template and add a new view as **RestaurantList.xaml**. The XAML in the view is a bit simpler than the previous view. Replace the templated view with the following:

```
<?xml version="1.0" encoding="UTF-8"?>
<ContentPage xmlns="http://xamarin.com/schemas/2014/forms"
             xmlns:x="http://schemas.microsoft.com/winfx/2009/xaml"
             xmlns:views="clr-namespace:IslandMenu.Views;assembly=IslandMenu"
             xmlns:translate="clr-namespace:IslandMenu.Resources;assembly=IslandMenu"
             Title="{translate:Translate AppName}"
             x:Class="IslandMenu.Views.RestaurantList">
  <ContentPage.Resources>
    <ResourceDictionary>
      <translate:ImageResourceConverter x:Key="imageResourceCvt" />
    </ResourceDictionary>
  </ContentPage.Resources>
  <ContentPage.Content>
    <Grid>
      <Image Opacity="0.5"
                              x:Name="img"
                              Source="{Binding ImageUrl, Converter={StaticResource
                                        imageResourceCvt}}"
                              Scale="1"
                              Aspect="AspectFill"/>
      <StackLayout Padding="10,10,10,0">
        <Grid HeightRequest="150">
          <Grid Style="{DynamicResource TitleBox}" >
            <StackLayout >
              <Label Text="{translate:Translate AppDescription}" Style="{DynamicResource
                  TitleStyle}"></Label>
              <Label Text="{Binding LastUpdate}" Style="{DynamicResource TitleStyleSmall}"
                  x:Name="LastUpdateLabel"></Label>
            </StackLayout>
          </Grid>
        </Grid>
        <ListView ItemsSource="{Binding .}"
                                      SeparatorVisibility="None"
                                      BackgroundColor="Transparent"
                                      SeparatorColor="#DFDFDF"
                                      HasUnevenRows="false"
                                      RowHeight="160"
```

```
                  ItemTapped="OnItemTapped" >
            <ListView.ItemTemplate>
              <DataTemplate>
                <ViewCell>
                  <views:RestaurantItem  />
                </ViewCell>
              </DataTemplate>
            </ListView.ItemTemplate>
          </ListView>
        </StackLayout>
      </Grid>
  </ContentPage.Content>
</ContentPage>
```

Starting at the top, you see the namespace declaration for the converters, just like the restaurant item view. There is one more namespace declaration:

```
xmlns:views="clr-namespace:IslandMenu.Views;assembly=IslandMenu"
```

This code allows this page to reference the restaurant item view that you just created. There is also a Title attribute defined:

```
Title="{translate:Translate AppName}"
```

This code should localize the title of the app when it is onscreen. As with the restaurant item view, you have XAML markup to load an image from the resource assembly, and the Translate extension is used to localize the text.

For the ListView definition, there is the following block of code:

```
<ListView ItemsSource="{Binding .}"
      SeparatorVisibility="None"
      BackgroundColor="Transparent"
      SeparatorColor="#DFDFDF"
      HasUnevenRows="false"
      RowHeight="160"
      ItemTapped="OnItemTapped">
  <ListView.ItemTemplate>
    <DataTemplate>
      <ViewCell>
        <views:RestaurantItem  />
      </ViewCell>
    </DataTemplate>
  </ListView.ItemTemplate>
</ListView>
```

RestaurantList code-behind

At runtime, the restaurant item view that you created is used where you have the views:RestaurantItem tag, and there is an event handler for ItemTapped. The handler is defined in the code-behind file named RestaurantList.xaml.cs.

Open up that file now. This is where you instantiate the view model and wire it up to the view. You can also define the event handler listed in the XAML page. Replace the default contents of the RestaurantList. xaml.cs file with the following:

```
using IslandMenu.Models;
using IslandMenu.ViewModels;
using Xamarin.Forms;
using Xamarin.Forms.Xaml;

namespace IslandMenu.Views
{
    [XamlCompilation(XamlCompilationOptions.Compile)]
    public partial class RestaurantList : ContentPage
    {
        RestaurantsViewModel vm;
        public RestaurantList()
        {
            InitializeComponent();

            vm = new RestaurantsViewModel {Navigation = Navigation};

            img.BindingContext = vm;
            LastUpdateLabel.BindingContext = vm;

            BindingContext = vm.Restaurants;
        }

        private async void OnItemTapped(object sender, ItemTappedEventArgs e)
        {
            Restaurant restaurant = e.Item as Restaurant;

            await this.Navigation.PushAsync(new MenuList(restaurant));

            ((ListView)sender).SelectedItem = null;
        }
    }
}
```

There's not a lot of code here. Notice the compiler attribute that is decorating the page class:

```
[XamlCompilation(XamlCompilationOptions.Compile)]
```

This attribute, which was added with Xamarin.Forms 2, allows the XAML to be compiled into intermediate language (IL) when you compile the project. Prior to Xamarin.Forms 2, when you created your views in XAML, they were stored in the app as XAML text and compiled and loaded at runtime.

When you add this attribute, the XAML compiler (XAMLC) compiles the view at compile time. Why should you do this? You get three immediate benefits with XAMLC:

- The XAML markup is compiled and validated at compile. Without the XAMLC step, errors in the XAML are not detected until you actually ran the app.

- Because the XAML is already compiled to IL, the time it takes to create and load a new view at runtime is faster.

- And you get a slightly smaller file size because the XAML files are no longer in the final build of the app.

Take a look at the sole property of the view model and the constructor:

```
RestaurantsViewModel vm;
public RestaurantList()
{
    InitializeComponent();

    vm = new RestaurantsViewModel {Navigation = Navigation};

    img.BindingContext = vm;
    LastUpdateLabel.BindingContext = vm;

    BindingContext = vm.Restaurants;
}
```

The view model is a property of the view. In the constructor of the view, the view model is created and gets passed in the Navigation property. The Navigation property is used to enable the menu items page to return back to the restaurant list page.

The view model is assigned as the BindingContext of the image and last update label controls. Remember that you set the localized value of the LastUpdate property in the GetRestaurants() method of the view model. Assigning the BindingContext of the label is the only code needed to set the Test property of that label to the current value of the LastUpdate property.

Set the BindContext of the page to the view model's Restaurants property, which binds the list of restaurants to the ListView control.

▒ **Note** You may have wondered why you didn't just assign the view model's Restaurants list directly to the ListView control. That process does work and is an acceptable way to accomplish the same result. The XAML data binding works in a hierarchy, and child controls inherit the data binding of their parents.

Finally, the OnItemTapped event handler is defined:

```
private async void OnItemTapped(object sender, ItemTappedEventArgs e)
{
    Restaurant restaurant = e.Item as Restaurant;

    await this.Navigation.PushAsync(new MenuList(restaurant));

    ((ListView)sender).SelectedItem = null;
}
```

This listing refers to code that has not been written yet (but is next on the agenda). The ListView passes the current item from its data binding as the Item property of the ItemTappedEventArgs parameter. That parameter is passed in as part of the event signature.

Assign the item using the as operator to make a safe cast to the type that you would get back. Then use the PushAsync() method of the Navigation property to push a new instance of the menu list while passing the selected restaurant to the menu list. It won't compile until after you create the menu list.

The last line clears the current selection of the ListView. This is a defensive programming practice. If the code had deleted the selected item when it was tapped, the selection would be invalid. Clearing the selection keeps the code from doing unexpected things. It probably wasn't needed for this example, but it's a good pattern to follow.

MenuListItem View

Now it's time to create the menu list that was just referenced from the restaurant list. Like the restaurant list, there are two files: one for the menu item and the other for the list. Start with the menu item. Following the same steps that was used for the restaurant item view, add a Forms Xaml View named **MenuListItem.xaml** to the Views folder.

Open up the newly created view and replace the default markup code with the following:

```
<?xml version="1.0" encoding="UTF-8"?>
<ContentView xmlns="http://xamarin.com/schemas/2014/forms"
             xmlns:x="http://schemas.microsoft.com/winfx/2009/xaml"
             xmlns:translate="clr-namespace:IslandMenu.Resources;assembly=IslandMenu"
             x:Class="IslandMenu.Views.MenuListItem">
  <ContentView.Content>
    <Grid Style="{DynamicResource MessageBox}">
      <StackLayout Padding="0,5">
        <Label Text="{Binding Name}" Style="{DynamicResource NameStyle}"/>
        <Label Text="{Binding Description}" Style="{DynamicResource DepartmentStyle}"/>
        <StackLayout Orientation="Horizontal">
          <Label Text="{translate:Translate Price}" Style="{DynamicResource DepartmentStyle}"/>
          <Label Text="{Binding PriceInEuros, StringFormat='{0:0.00}'}"
              Style="{DynamicResource DepartmentStyle}"/>
          <Label Text="{translate:Translate EUR}" Style="{DynamicResource DepartmentStyle}"/>
        </StackLayout>
        <BoxView Style="{DynamicResource ShadowStyle}"></BoxView>
      </StackLayout>
    </Grid>
  </ContentView.Content>
</ContentView>
```

This is fairly straightforward and does only one new thing. Take a look at the data binding for the price control:

```
<Label Text="{Binding PriceInEuros, StringFormat='{0:0.00}'}" Style="{DynamicResource DepartmentStyle}"/>
```

In addition to binding the value of the PriceInEuros property to the Text property of the Label control, you are using the StringFormat of the Binding to manipulate the value of the PriceInEuros property.

StringFormat works very much like String.Format, with a couple of differences: the format string is enclosed inside single quote characters, and the placeholder for the property value is always 0. The "0.00" format mask formats the value as a number with two decimal places and uses the current culture's decimal point character. For some cultures, the decimal point character is ".", and the numbers would look like 1.23 or 19.10. Other cultures use "," because the decimal placeholder and the two previous values would display as 1,23 and 19,10. The StringFormat attribute lets the app easily handle cultural formatting in the XAML markup code.

MenuList View

With the menu item defined, you can now define the menu list. Add a Forms Xaml page and name it **MenuList.xaml**. As with the other XAML files, replace the default contents with the following:

```
<?xml version="1.0" encoding="UTF-8"?>
<ContentPage xmlns="http://xamarin.com/schemas/2014/forms"
             xmlns:x="http://schemas.microsoft.com/winfx/2009/xaml"
             xmlns:views="clr-namespace:IslandMenu.Views;assembly=IslandMenu"
             xmlns:translate="clr-namespace:IslandMenu.Resources;assembly=IslandMenu"
             x:Class="IslandMenu.Views.MenuList">
  <ContentPage.Resources>
    <ResourceDictionary>
      <translate:ImageResourceConverter x:Key="imageResourceCvt" />
    </ResourceDictionary>
  </ContentPage.Resources>
  <ContentPage.Content>
    <Grid>
      <StackLayout Padding="10,10,10,10">
        <Grid HeightRequest="200">
          <Image Opacity="0.75"
                 x:Name="img1"
                 Source="{Binding Photo, Converter={StaticResource imageResourceCvt}}"
                 Scale="1"
                 Aspect="AspectFill"/>
          <Grid Style="{DynamicResource TitleBox}">
            <StackLayout Spacing="1">
              <Label Text="{Binding Name}" Style="{DynamicResource TitleStyle}"></Label>
              <Label Text="{Binding Address1}" Style="{DynamicResource TitleStyleSmall}"></Label>
              <StackLayout Orientation="Horizontal" HorizontalOptions="FillAndExpand">
                <Label Text="{Binding Town}" Style="{DynamicResource TitleStyleSmall}"></Label>
                <Label Text="{Binding PhoneNumber}" Style="{DynamicResource TitleStyleSmall}"
                       HorizontalOptions="EndAndExpand"></Label>
              </StackLayout>
            </StackLayout>
          </Grid>
        </Grid>

        <ListView ItemsSource="{Binding Menu}"
                  SeparatorVisibility="None"
                  BackgroundColor="Transparent"
                  SeparatorColor="#DFDFDF"
                  HasUnevenRows="True"
                  RowHeight="100">
          <ListView.ItemTemplate>
            <DataTemplate>
              <ViewCell BindingContextChanged="OnBindingContextChanged">
                <views:MenuListItem  />
              </ViewCell>
            </DataTemplate>
          </ListView.ItemTemplate>
```

```
        </ListView>
      </StackLayout>
    </Grid>
  </ContentPage.Content>
</ContentPage>
```

This is very similar in design to the way the data binding for the menu list was defined. If you look at the ListView, there are two new things: the HasUnEvenRows property of the ListView is set to true. And the ViewCell is a little different:

```
<ViewCell BindingContextChanged="OnBindingContextChanged">
  <views:MenuListItem  />
</ViewCell>
```

You have assigned an event handler to the BindingContextChanged event. This event gets fired for each new row in the list. It is used to change the height of the ListView cell when the menu item description is wide enough to word wrap onto another line.

░ **Note**   Your layout should be flexible enough to handle string lengths that are longer than what you expected. When translating a sentence to another language, the translated sentence may be quite a bit longer than the original text. For example, the English phrase "My friend is a nervous passenger" could be translated as "Lu ma 'amicu è un passageru incheta Diana" in the Corsican language. That's almost ten characters longer.

MenuList Code-behind

With the XAML part of the menu list defined, you need to add some code to the code-behind file. Open up the MenuList.xaml.cs file and replace the default code with the following:

```
using System;
using IslandMenu.Models;
using Xamarin.Forms;
using Xamarin.Forms.Xaml;

namespace IslandMenu.Views
{
    [XamlCompilation(XamlCompilationOptions.Compile)]
    public partial class MenuList : ContentPage
    {
        public MenuList(Restaurant restaurant)
        {
            BindingContext = restaurant;
            this.Title = restaurant.Name;
            InitializeComponent();
        }

        private void OnBindingContextChanged(object sender, EventArgs e)
        {
            base.OnBindingContextChanged();
```

```
            var cell = (ViewCell) sender;
            RestaurantMenuItem item = (RestaurantMenuItem)cell.BindingContext;

            var l = item.Description.Length;
            var offset = (l / 50) * 20;

            cell.Height = 100 + offset;
        }
    }
}
```

This is very similar to the other code-behind changes. Look at the constructor:

```
public MenuList(Restaurant restaurant)
{
    BindingContext = restaurant;
    this.Title = restaurant.Name;
    InitializeComponent();
}
```

When this page is created from the restaurant list, it was passed the currently selected restaurant. In the constructor, that restaurant is assigned as the BindingContent for the page. You also set the Title property of the page to the restaurant name.

The only other code in this class is the event handler for the BindContextChanged event, which gets fired for each cell when it is instantiated:

```
private void OnBindingContextChanged(object sender, EventArgs e)
{
    base.OnBindingContextChanged();

    var cell = (ViewCell) sender;
    RestaurantMenuItem item = (RestaurantMenuItem)cell.BindingContext;

    var l = item.Description.Length;
    var offset = (l / 50) * 20;

    cell.Height = 100 + offset;
}
```

This code casts the sender parameter as a ViewCell. From the ViewCell, it can cast the BindingContext as the current RestaurantMenuItem. Once it has a reference to the selected RestaurantMenuItem, it can check the length of its Description property and adjust the height accordingly. This is an extremely easy way to determine the display length of a string, but it is close enough for demo purposes. The actual length depends on the font and the actual text.

Wiring Up the View

Now that you have the models, the views, and the view model, there is just one more bit of code necessary to wire it up. Open up the `App.xaml.cs` file. The default constructor should look a little bit like this:

```
public App()
{
    InitializeComponent();

    MainPage = new IslandMenu.MainPage();
}
```

The `MainPage` object is the default page created by the Xamarin project template. Change that code to the following:

```
public App()
{
    InitializeComponent();

    MainPage = new NavigationPage(new Views.RestaurantList());
}
```

The code is changed to create an instance of the `RestaurantList,` which gives it the capability to handle the navigation to other pages.

Running the Code

You should be able to compile and the run the code. If it doesn't compile, just take the completed project from [INSERT SOURCE CODE URL HERE] and follow along that code. The running Island Menu on Android looks like Figure 4-1 after it loads.

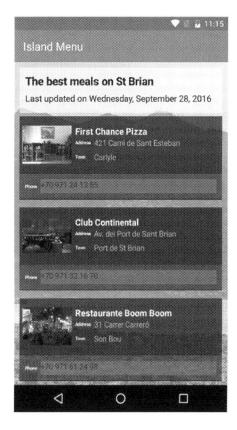

Figure 4-1. *Restaurant list on Android*

If you tap the First Chance Pizza item, you see the page shown in Figure 4-2.

Figure 4-2. Menu list on Android

For iOS, you see something like the page in Figure 4-3.

Figure 4-3. *Restaurant list on the iPhone*

For Windows 10 Phone, you see something like the page in Figure 4-4.

Figure 4-4. Restaurant list on Windows 10 Mobile

And for a Windows 10 Desktop application, you see the page shown in Figure 4-5.

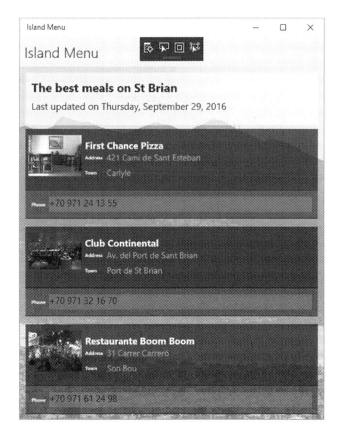

Figure 4-5. *Restaurant list on Windows 10 Desktop*

Running the UWP desktop app looks just like the Windows 10 Mobile version, but with the addition of the miminize, maximize, and close buttons. A Windows 10 UWP compiled with Xamarin.Forms runs the same code on the PC and the phone.

Note The Android and Windows screenshots were taken from the Windows 10 and Android emulators that come with Visual Studio. The iPhone screenshot was taken with the Xamarin iOS Simulator for Windows.

Localizing the App

Now that the app works on each platform in English, it's time to provide support for some additional languages. You will add Spanish, German, and Chinese (Simplified).

You can use the MAT to generate the additional resource files. For the purposes of this example, the MAT machine will translate the files. You would not want to ship an app that was machine translated, but this gets you one step closer. It takes care of the string resources in the resource file.

Translating the data file is a bit tricky. In a real application, the data would have come from some database, already translated for you. In this case, the code uses JSON files embedded in the app. You can make translated versions for each language. The completed app at [INSERT SOURCE URL HERE] has copies of the translated files for you to use.

The completed app has translations that were done by professionals. The Spanish translation was by Maximiliano Diaz through SmartCAT (`www.smartcat.ai/`). Максим Морковкин did the Chinese translation, also through SmartCAT. The German translation was done by David Krings, a co-worker of the author and native German speaker.

▓ **Note**   The value that a human translation adds to your app can't be overemphasized. It is the difference between having an app that feels native to the user to one that just doesn't feel right.

Using the MAT

Make sure that the Island Menu PCL project is the currently selected project. It doesn't have to be the startup project; it just needs to be the selected one. From the Tools menu, select Multilingual App Toolkit and then select Enable Selection.

Now add the additional languages to the project. From the Project menu, select Multilingual App Toolkit and then Add Translation Languages. When the Translation Languages dialog appears, select Chinese (Simplified [zh-Hans], German [de], and Spanish [es]. Press OK to add the languages to the project.

This demo project uses single dialects of each language, which eliminates the need to create language and country locale versions, such as es-MX for the Mexican dialect of Spanish.

The MultilingualResources folder is created for the project, so add the XLF files to the folder. Right-click the MultilingualResources folder and select Multilingual App Toolkit and then Generate Machine Translations. Each XLF file is then translated by the Microsoft translation services.

The next step is to compile or rebuild the project, which creates or updates the RESX files for the additional languages.

For the data files, you need to have `data-es.json`, `data-de.json`, and `data-zh.json`. You can translate them manually by copying the English `data.json` file and doing the translation yourself or just take the translated files from the completed app.

When you run the app now on a device or emulator set up for Spanish, the Restaurant list looks like Figure 4-6.

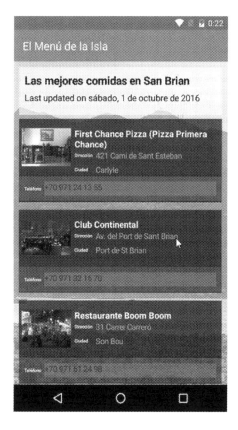

Figure 4-6. *Restaurant list in Spanish*

The title now appears in Spanish. The Last updated… string that you updated in code is also translated into Spanish, as are the labels on the list. Most of the rest of the text that is associated the restaurants is still in the original language. If you were looking for the restaurant when you were on St. Brian, you would be looking for it in the original language (see Figure 4-7).

Figure 4-7. *Menu list in Spanish*

For the menu items, the description of the item has been translated to the user's language. The name of the menu item is in both the original language and the translated language, which makes it easier for the user to order that dish at the restaurant. The numeric formatting of the price now matches the country setting from the user's preferences.

If you change the language to German and run the app, you'll see the text strings replaced with the German translation, as shown in Figure 4-8.

Figure 4-8. *Restaurant list in German*

There is one more language translation, Chinese (Simplified), as shown in Figure 4-9.

Figure 4-9. *Restaurant list in Chinese (Simplified)*

Platform Specifics

Although resource files and JSON files handle the translations within the app, they don't handle everything. The name of the app as it appears on the device has to be localized at the platform level. The text and media resources for each app store have to be translated separately from the app itself.

Android

You can use the Android style of string localization to properly localize the name of the app. It is the source for the text that appears in the Android launcher.

Select the Resources folder of the IslandMenu.Droid project. There should be a values folder inside the Resources folder. Add the following folders: values-de, values-es, and values-zh. If you create folders for country versions of a language, remember to include an *r* in front of the country code (e.g. values-es-rMX for Mexican Spanish).

Add a `strings.xml` file to the values folder. You'll create an Android style string resource that can be used for the application name. Technically, it sets the display label of the main activity, but that's how it works on Android. Use the following for the contents of the `string.xml` file:

```
<?xml version="1.0" encoding="utf-8" ?>
<resources>
  <string name="app_name">Island Menu</string>
</resources>
```

You have to create the same file in the values-de, values-es, and values-zh folders. Use the same value from the AppName string in the RESX file for each language in the portable library project. For example, the strings.xml file in the values-de folder looks something like this:

```
<?xml version="1.0" encoding="utf-8" ?>
<resources>
  <string name="app_name">Menú Isla</string>
</resources>
```

Open the MainActivity.cs file from the IslandMenu.Droid project. This is the Android activity that gets run when the Android app starts up. It has the code to initialize and run the Xamarin.Forms code.

Above the definition of the MainActivity class are some attributes. Xamarin uses .NET style attributes as way to set activity properties that would otherwise need to go in the AndroidManifest.xml file. It should look something like this:

```
[Activity(Label = "IslandMenu", Icon = "@drawable/icon", Theme = "@style/MainTheme",
MainLauncher = true, ConfigurationChanges = ConfigChanges.ScreenSize | ConfigChanges.
Orientation)]
```

The Label attribute needs to change. Replace the "IslandMenu" string with "@string/app_name". The @string token tells Android to look in the string resources and get the value for the string resource named app_name. The attribute should now look like this:

```
[Activity(Label = "@string/app_name", Icon = "@drawable/icon", Theme = "@style/MainTheme",
MainLauncher = true, ConfigurationChanges = ConfigChanges.ScreenSize | ConfigChanges.
Orientation)]
```

After making that change, rebuild the IslandMenu.Droid project. If you have a device or emulator running in one of the languages that the the IslandMenu app now supports, when you run the app, you will see the text in the translated language.

The app should run just as it did before; the difference is the way the app appears on the Android launcher. Before localizing the Label of the MainActivity, the name of the app would always appear as Island Menu (see Figure 4-10).

Figure 4-10. *Island Menu in Android launcher, English*

After making that change, the name of the app will now be displayed with the translated name in the Android Launcher as shown in Figure 4-11.

Figure 4-11. *Island Menu in Android launcher, Spanish*

It also appears in the recent app list with the localized name, as shown in Figure 4-12.

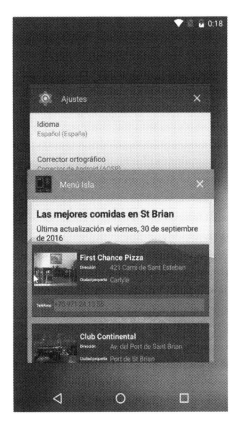

Figure 4-12. *Island Menu in Android Recent Apps List, Spanish*

iOS

With iOS, the localization is handled a little differently. There are predefined string names in iOS for items such as the app title. You need to set the localized value for `CFBundleDisplayName`, which is a predefined variable name used by iOS and macOS to define the display name of your app. It's used on the home screen, in the Settings app, and also by Siri.

Select the IslandMenu.iOS project. Select the Resources folder and add the following folders: de.lproj, es.lproj, and zh.lproj. In each of the lproj folders, add a text file named `InfoPlist.string`.

Select the es.lproj folder and add the `InfoPlist.string` text file. Open the file and put in the following text:

```
"CFBundleDisplayName" = "Menú Isla";
```

Do the same process for the other lproj folders; it localizes the name of the app as it is displayed on the iOS Springboard launcher.

Windows UWP

With UWP applications, you localize the name and the description of the app. The structure is similar to the way Android and iOS handle their string resources. Because this is an UWP app, you have to use the `.resw` resource format instead of the `.resx` format.

▪ **Note** Starting with Windows 8 Store Apps, Microsoft changed the way localized resources were bundled with the application. With that change, the `.resw` file extension was introduced. The `.resw` file format is identical to the `.resx` format, except that it stores only strings and file paths.

Select the IslandMenu.UWP app, right-click the project, and add a folder named **Strings**. Create the following folders inside the Strings folder: de, en-US, es, and zh-Hans.

In the en-US folder, right-click the folder; select Add and then New Item. Select the Resources File (.resw) template and use the default name Resources.resw. It should look like Figure 4-13.

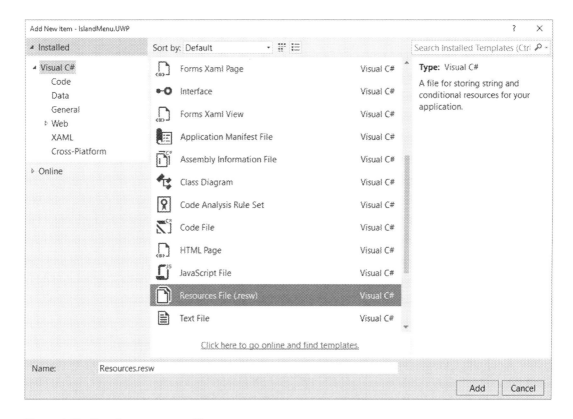

Figure 4-13. *Creating a new .resw file*

Press Add to add the resource file. After the file is created, double-click the file to edit it. The resource editor displays, which looks like the same editor that you used on the .resx files.

Add two string resources and name them **"AppName"** and **"AppDescription"**. Use the same values from the .resx file in the PCL project. The end result should look like Figure 4-14.

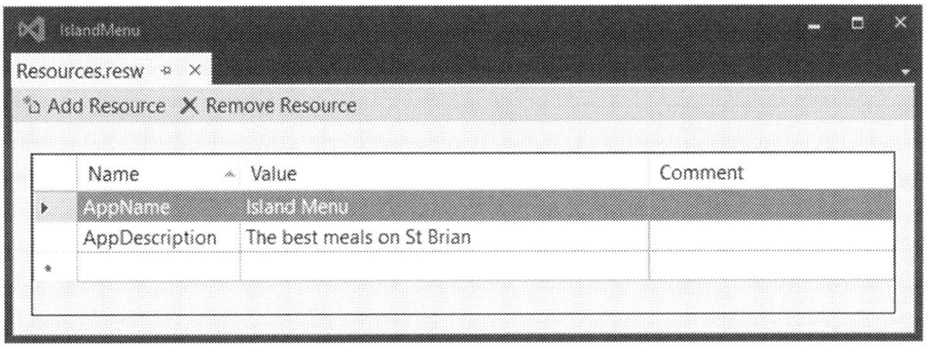

Figure 4-14. *Resources.resw for Windows 10 UWP in English*

Next, add Resources.resw files for the de, es, and zh-Hans folders. Use the same "AppName" and "AppDescription" strings and copy the values from the .resx files for each language in the PCL project. For example, the Resources.resx file in the es folder should look like Figure 4-15.

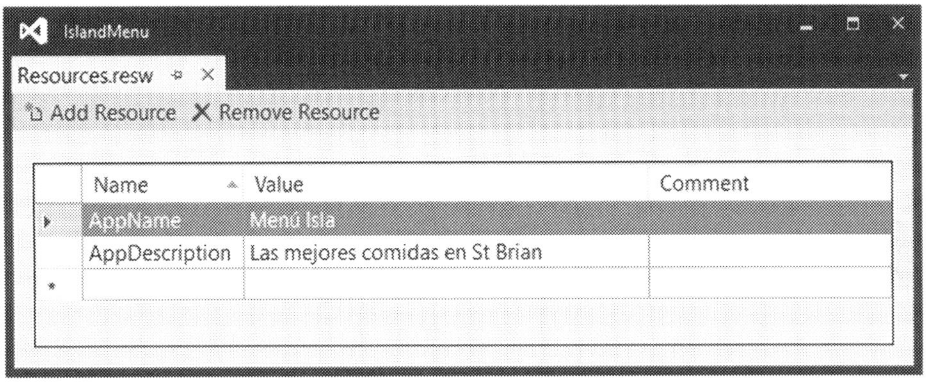

Figure 4-15. *Resources.resw for Windows 10 UWP in Spanish*

Now that the fields are localized, you need to update the app manifest to use the values from the resource files. Right-click the project file and select Properties. When the Properties page opens up, select the Application tab on the left side, and then press the Package Manifest button. A file named Package.appxmanifest opens.

On the Application tab, set the value of the Display Name field to ms-resource:AppName and change the value of the Description field to ms-Resource:AppDescription. The manifest page should look like Figure 4-16.

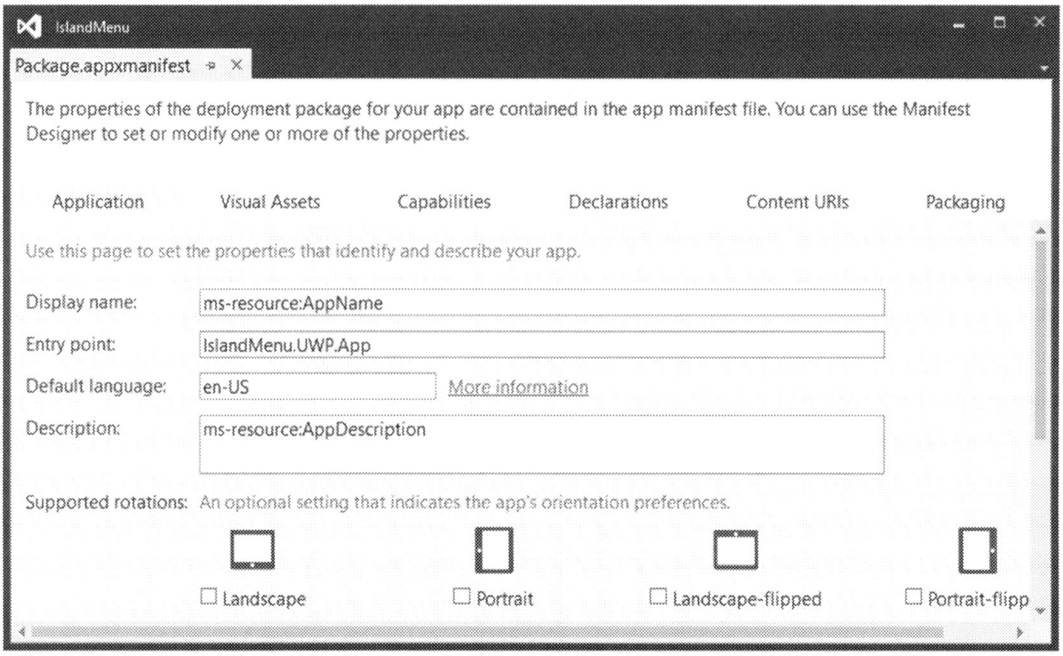

Figure 4-16. *Resources.resw referenced in the Windows 10 UWP app manifest*

Now you can compile and run the app. If you have a Windows 10 emulator set up for Spanish, the name should now show up translated. If you right-swipe in the emulator to bring up the app list, the name should be right at the top and look like Figure 4-17.

Figure 4-17. *Viewing the localized app name on Windows 10 UWP*

Wrapping Up

You just built a simple app from scratch, and it wasn't that hard to set it up to support multiple languages. Even though the app was compiled for three wildly different OSs, almost all the code was in a shared PCL.

The only code that was platform specific was the code to handle displaying the app name correctly on each platform. Everything else came from a single set of shared resources.

▓ **Note** Always do a spot check of your application with a language that is different from your default language. Text that was not translated or localized is very apparent and it makes it very easy to find any part of the app that didn't get fully localized.

CHAPTER 5

▨ ▨ ▨

Additional Resources

"County library? Reference desk, please. Hello? Yes, I need a word definition. Well, that's
the problem. I don't know how to spell it and I'm not allowed to say it. Could you just rattle
off all the swear words you know and I'll stop you when . . . Hello?"

—Bill Watterson, "Calvin and Hobbes"

About Xamarin.Forms

To write the sample app in Chapter 4, you used Xamarin.Forms to write code that is shared across the multiple platforms. Xamarin.Forms is a product from Xamarin, a subsidiary of Microsoft.

Xamarin is a company that ported the Microsoft .NET Framework to iOS and Android. It enables you to write fast, native applications in the C# and F# languages. Although the UI code for each platform is specific to each platform, the business logic of the app can be shared across platforms. Microsoft acquired Xamarin in 2016, and it is now part of the Microsoft Visual Studio development tools.

If you do not already own a copy of Visual Studio 2015, Microsoft has a free version for students, open-source development teams, and individual developers. This version, the Community edition, includes the Xamarin tools. It can be downloaded from `www.visualstudio.com/downloads/`.

Xamarin.Forms is a library that lets you write code to run on Android, iOS, and Windows with shared UI code. It provides an abstraction layer for the UI. Instead of using the native UI controls directly, you reference the Xamarin.Forms version of the controls. At runtime, the native controls are used. To learn more about Xamarin.Forms, please see the online documentation provided by Xamarin at `https://developer.xamarin.com/guides/xamarin-forms/`.

If you prefer to use Xamarin.Android, Xamarin.iOS, or UWP for Windows, most of this book still applies. Instead of a set of `.resx` files in the shared library, you can still create the platform native string resource file for your default language. For Android, it is the `Strings.xml` file in the Resource/values folder. For iOS, you have the `Localizable.strings` file in the Resources/Base.lproj folder. For UWP, you create the default `.resw` file in the Strings/en-US folder.

Once you have the platform-specific resource files working for your default language, you can enable the Multilingual App Toolkit (MAT) for each platform. You can then add the languages; that process creates the XLF files in each project. Once you translate the XLF, either through machine translation or by a professional, the MAT creates the native files for each platform.

Going full native instead of using Xamarin.Forms works just fine with the MAT, but you have multiple sets of XLF files to manage. You do have the option of using a shared PCL with the native Xamarin.Android, Xamarin.iOS, and UWP projects, which enables you to have a single source for the strings.

If you use a cross-platform MVVM library such as Mvvm Light (`www.mvvmlight.net/`), Prism (`https://github.com/PrismLibrary/Prism`), or MvvmCross (`https://mvvmcross.com/`), you can share most of the UI code across the platforms and make good use of the shared `.resx` files.

© Christopher Miller 2017
C. Miller, *Cross-platform Localization for Native Mobile Apps with Xamarin*,
DOI 10.1007/978-1-4842-2466-3_5

Emulators

When debugging and testing your app, you should use emulators as much as possible. Using mobile device emulators lets you run on more device sizes than you could ever possibly own. You can also pick and choose which OS versions to test on.

Note Strictly speaking, the iOS emulator isn't actually an emulator, it's a simulator. An emulator works by emulating the behavior of the device. An emulated device runs the actual mobile OS and apps as if they were on a real device. The hardware of the device is emulated, but appears to be (and behaves as if) it is real. The iOS simulator provides a simulated view of the operating, but does not actually emulate the device hardware. This is why you can download apps from Google Play into an Android emulator, but you can't download apps from the iTunes App store into the iOS Simulator.

Another advantage of using an emulator: you can easily change the language and region for a device and not have to worry about knowing the language enough to change it back to the default. You can also run multiple Android emulators side by side and have them in different languages and regions. It's a good way to check your app for fit and finish issues when working with translated languages.

With Visual Studio 2015, you have the option of installing the Visual Studio Emulator for Android. You can also install the emulator by downloading it from `www.visualstudio.com/vs/msft-android-emulator/`.

Locale

The standard code for languages is the ISO 639 set of standards. You'll typically use the ISO 639-1 set of codes, each of which has two characters. A second set of three-character codes for languages is defined as ISO 639-2.

Some languages do not have a two-character ISO 639-1 code; they have the three-character ISO 639-2 code instead. For those languages, use the ISO 639-2 code. For example, suppose that you are doing apps localized to use Native American languages such as Cherokee or Cheyenne. They do not have ISO 639-1 codes, but have ISO 639-1 codes, so you use "chr" and "chy" (respectively) for the two languages.

Note To see a full list of ISO 639 codes, access the Wikipedia article "List of ISO 639-2 Codes" located at `https://en.wikipedia.org/wiki/List_of_ISO_639-2_codes`.

Country codes are defined as part of the ISO 3166 standard. The two-character codes used to represent country or region in the locale string are defined as ISO 639-2. A list of ISO 3166-2 codes can be found in the Wikipedia article "ISO 3166-2," which can be accessed at `https://en.wikipedia.org/wiki/ISO_3166-2`.

Currency

Although this book did not provide a sample of using a currency rate exchange, there are both free and commercial services that can be accessed from a mobile app. Table 5-1 shows selected free and commercial sites that offer "forex" exchange services.

Table 5-1. *List of Selected ForEx Services*

Name	License	URL
European Central Bank	Free	`https://www.ecb.europa.eu/stats/exchange/eurofxref/html/index.en.html`
Forcefeed.net	Paid	`http://forexfeed.net/forex-data-services`
OANDA	Paid	`https://www.oanda.com`
Open Exchange Rate	Free/Paid	`https://openexchangerates.org`
Xignite	Paid	`http://www.xignite.com/forex`

When converting currency, let the user know that the conversion rate is an approximate value. The actual conversion rate they get when they exchange their money will be different and might include some fees.

The European Central Bank has a page that has foreign exchange rates against the euro. The page is updated once per day and can be found at `www.ecb.europa.eu/stats/exchange/eurofxref/html/index.en.html`. There is an XML version of the page that contains just the reference rates; access it at `www.ecb.europa.eu/stats/eurofxref/eurofxref-daily.xml`. A recent download of the daily rate looks like this:

```xml
<?xml version="1.0" encoding="UTF-8"?>
<gesmes:Envelope xmlns:gesmes="http://www.gesmes.org/xml/2002-08-01" xmlns="http://www.ecb.int/vocabulary/2002-08-01/eurofxref">
        <gesmes:subject>Reference rates</gesmes:subject>
        <gesmes:Sender>
                <gesmes:name>European Central Bank</gesmes:name>
        </gesmes:Sender>
        <Cube>
                <Cube time='2016-09-30'>
                        <Cube currency='USD' rate='1.1161'/>
                        <Cube currency='JPY' rate='113.09'/>
                        <Cube currency='BGN' rate='1.9558'/>
                        <Cube currency='CZK' rate='27.021'/>
                        <Cube currency='DKK' rate='7.4513'/>
                        <Cube currency='GBP' rate='0.86103'/>
                        <Cube currency='HUF' rate='309.79'/>
                        <Cube currency='PLN' rate='4.3192'/>
                        <Cube currency='RON' rate='4.4537'/>
                        <Cube currency='SEK' rate='9.6210'/>
                        <Cube currency='CHF' rate='1.0876'/>
                        <Cube currency='NOK' rate='8.9865'/>
                        <Cube currency='HRK' rate='7.5220'/>
                        <Cube currency='RUB' rate='70.5140'/>
                        <Cube currency='TRY' rate='3.3576'/>
                        <Cube currency='AUD' rate='1.4657'/>
                        <Cube currency='BRL' rate='3.6210'/>
                        <Cube currency='CAD' rate='1.4690'/>
                        <Cube currency='CNY' rate='7.4463'/>
                        <Cube currency='HKD' rate='8.6547'/>
                        <Cube currency='IDR' rate='14566.22'/>
                        <Cube currency='ILS' rate='4.1996'/>
```

```
                    <Cube currency='INR' rate='74.3655'/>
                    <Cube currency='KRW' rate='1229.76'/>
                    <Cube currency='MXN' rate='21.7389'/>
                    <Cube currency='MYR' rate='4.6148'/>
                    <Cube currency='NZD' rate='1.5369'/>
                    <Cube currency='PHP' rate='54.015'/>
                    <Cube currency='SGD' rate='1.5235'/>
                    <Cube currency='THB' rate='38.695'/>
                    <Cube currency='ZAR' rate='15.5238'/>
            </Cube>
        </Cube>
</gesmes:Envelope>
```

Based on that document, if you want to display 50 euros in Chinese yuan, do the following:

1. Request the current rates by downloading the XML document.

2. Get the euro–to-yuan exchange rate by searching on the three-letter code for Chinese yuan (CNY). For this download, that rate is 7.4463.

3. Multiple the 50 euros by that rate to get a value of 372.32 yuan.

To convert from U.S. dollars to Chinese yuan, multiply the dollar value by the euro-to-yuan rate and then divide that result by the euro-to-dollar rate. You have to display the correct currency symbols.

Pluralization

Although your best option is to use a layout that avoids pluralization rules, you may sometimes have to pluralize some of your text. A good reference that lists the different plural rules by language is maintained by the Mozilla project in its developer documentation. This page, "Localization and Plurals," can be accessed at `https://developer.mozilla.org/en-US/docs/Mozilla/Localization/Localization_and_Plurals`.

The Mozilla reference defines 16 rules. For example, rule #2 as defined by Mozilla has two forms and applies to French and Brazilian Portuguese. Form 1 applies to the quantities 0 or 1; form 2 is for everything else.

For those two languages, you need two resource strings. For example, suppose that you want to display a message when one or more files are uploaded. For French, you can use the the following for forms 1 and 2:

```
"{0} fichier téléchargé"
"{0} fichiers téléchargés"
```

Most of the other European languages use plural rule #1, which also has two rules. Form 1 applies to the quantity 1; form 2 is for everything else. For Spanish, you can define the following two resource strings for the forms:

```
"{0} archivo subido"
"{0} archivos subidos"
```

If you had a resource file named `MyResource`, you could have resource strings named "Upload1" and "Upload2" that have the strings that would be correct for form 1 and form 2. If you supported languages that had more forms, you would define strings for each one. You would have one more resource string called "PluralRule". Set that string to the rule number for that language. For `MyResource.es.rex`, the value of "PluralRule" would be 1.

Create a descendant class of MyResource and call it MyResourceHelper. You can add public methods to return the correct plural string and add some private methods to make the work easier and reusable. You can add that class to the same namespace as the MyResource class, which looks something like this:

```
public class MyResourceHelper : MyResource
{
        public static string GetPluralForUpload(int quantity)
        {
                var form = GetFormForQuantity(quantity);
                var tmp = ResourceManager.GetString($"Upload{form}", MyResource.Culture);
                return String.Format(tmp, quantity);
        }

        public static int GetFormForQuantity(int quantity)
        {
                var rule = Convert.ToInt32(MyResource.PluralRule);

                // default form for every rule, for rule 0 it's the only form
                var form = 1;

                switch (rule)
                {
                        case 1:
                                if (quantity != 1)
                                        form = 2;
                                break;
                        case 2:
                                if (quantity > 1)
                                        form = 2;
                                break;
                        case 3:
                                if (quantity == 0)
                                {
                                        form = 1;
                                }
                                else if (EndsWithN(quantity, 1) && (quantity != 11))
                                {
                                        form = 2;
                                }
                                else
                                        form = 3;
                                break;
                        // define other rules & forms
                }

                return form;
        }
        private static bool EndsWithN(int value, int EndNum)
        {
                return (value % 10 == EndNum);
        }
}
```

Use this helper by calling it like this, where n is the quantity that you need to pluralize:

```
var someString = MyResourceHelper.GetPluralForUpload(n);
```

The GetFormForQuantity() method takes the quantity and checks to see which PluralRule applies to the current language. Then it just uses a simple set of rules to see which form is needed.

Once you have the form number, you can make a string with the form number to match the resource strings that have been defined. You then call the ResourceManager.GetString() method with the resource string name that was just constructed and the current culture, which comes from the resource class.

The parameterized string (such as "{0} archivo subido") is returned and then passed to String.Format() with the quantity. The return value is the localized string with the correct plural format.

It's a little complicated to set up, but once you have it in place, it is easy to create additional plural strings.

Vernacular

Long-time Xamarin users have had another option for localization. Software team members at Rdio created their own localization tools under the name Vernacular. They provide command-line tools to parse the source code and generate .pot files. You then send the .pot files to a translation service and get back .po files, one for each supported language. The command-line tool then takes the .po file and generates the platform-specific string resource files.

POT, which stands for *portable object template*, contains the strings to be translated, where the string appears in the code, and hint information. The hint information provides context to the translator. PO, which stands for *portable object*, is the translated version of the POT file, with one .po file for each of the languages being translated to. Although the POT and PO files sound like they might be different formats, they do use the same format.

Vernacular provides an API inspired by gettext and has support for both pluralization and genders. The gettext library was originally developed by Sun Microsystems to handle localization in Unix applications. GNU gettext is an open-source version that was released in 1995.

With gettext, the .po files are compiled to a binary file with either an .mo or .gmo (GNU gettext) extension. The gettext() function takes a string token and replaces it with the translated version from the .mo file.

Vernacular uses the platform string resource files instead of the .mo files. The same command-line tool that generates the .pot file from the source code is also used to generate the resource files from the .po files. In Vernacular terminology, this step is called the Merge step.

The workflow flows roughly like this. The first step is called the Extract step. You run the Vernacular command-line executable against the input files and create the .pot file. A sample run can look like this:

```
$ vernacular       \
        --output=project.pot \
        --input=bin/Debug \
        --input=Resources/Values/strings.xml \
        --source-root=$PWD \
        --generator=po \
        --pot \
        --meta="Project-Id-Version=Sample Project" \
        --meta="POT-Creation-Date=$(date '+%Y-%m-%d       %H:%M%z')" \
        --analyze \
        --analyzer-config=vernacular-analyzer.xml
```

For ease of formatting, use this syntax in a Mac terminal session. It generates a .pot file named project.pot and uses the compiled debug assemblies for the app and the default strings.xml file. Once you have the .pot file, you can edit it and add comments where appropriate.

Send the .pot file out to be translated and get back a set of .po files, one for each language that was translated. (This example assumes that the translation people added the language code to the file name.) Then run the Vernacular command as the Merge step. To generate the French language resource file on iOS, run the command like this:

```
$ vernacular \
        --output=fr.lproj/Localizable.strings \
        --input=project_FR.po \
        --generator=ios
```

You have to run it for each language and for each platform. Ideally, you script these steps with MSBuild.

Use Vernacular.Catalog as the API for localizing the strings in code. Using the "files downloaded" example from the previous section, you could have a .pot file named project.pot that includes the following entries:

```
#. TRANSLATORS: This describes the number of files to be uploaded msgid "{0} file
downloaded"
msgstr ""

msgid "{0} files downloaded"
msgstr ""
```

The French translation, named project-fr.po, includes the following:

```
#. TRANSLATORS: This describes the number of files to be uploaded
msgid "{0} file downloaded"
msgstr "{0} fichier téléchargé"

msgid "{0} files downloaded"
msgstr "{0} fichiers téléchargés"
```

Using the "files downloaded" example from the previous section, the Vernacular code looks like this:

```
var labelString = Catalog.GetPluralString(
    "{0} file downloaded",
    "{0} files downloaded",
    filecount);
```

There are some advantages to using Vernacular. It has support for plurals and genders, and has the tooling to make it a cross-platform solution. With gettext being around since 1995, it's a well-known tool, and translation companies are very familiar with it.

There are some potential disadvantages. Vernacular has a very nice API and tooling, but it was developed by a company that unfortunately went out of business. Documentation is scarce, and you need to understand how the command-line tools work in order to build your applications.

Vernacular is an open-source project hosted on Github at https://github.com/rdio/vernacular.

XLIFF

Professional translation services can work with a file format called XLIFF, which stands for *XML Localization Interchange File Format*. It was created to provide a standard file format for localization conversion tools. The MAT uses XLIFF as a storage format. The MAT provides enough functionality with its editor; you should never have to edit the XLIFF files manually. If you send the XLIFF files out to be translated, you should be able to replace the existing files in your project with the updated files.

An XLIFF file typically uses an `.xlf` file extension and is based on XML. It's designed to be used by translation tools and is not very human readable. In addition to storing the translated text, the XLIFF file allows you to store the state of a translation. When an item of text is translated, an attribute named `state` can be associated with the text translation. You can flag text items as new, `translated`, `translated but needs review`, `signed off`, and a few other states.

A well-defined XML format allows tools from different suppliers to read and write to the same format. Different tools can add their own extensions, and those extensions are relevant only to that tool. Other tools skip over extensions that they don't recognize.

As defined in the OASIS XLIFF Core Spec (`http://docs.oasis-open.org/xliff/xliff-core/xliff-core.html`), the predefined values for states (`http://docs.oasis-open.org/xliff/v1.2/os/xliff-core.html#state`) are defined in Table 5-2.

Table 5-2. *XLIFF 1.2 States*

Value	Description
final	Indicates the terminating state.
needs-adaptation	Indicates that only nontextual information needs adaptation.
needs-l10n	Indicates that both text and nontextual information needs adaptation.
needs-review-adaptation	Indicates that only nontextual information needs review.
needs-review-l10n	Indicates that both text and nontextual information needs review.
needs-review-translation	Indicates that only the text of the item needs review.
needs-translation	Indicates that the item needs to be translated.
new	Indicates that the item is new (for example, a translation unit that wasn't in a previous version of the document).
signed-off	Indicates that changes are reviewed and approved.
translated	Indicates that the item has been translated.

Additional values can be defined by XLIFF tool vendors. The value names for vendor-specific items start with *x-*. The version of MAT current at the time of this writing ignores custom values.

The `state` attribute lets you manage the translation process for each item, which allows you to add or edit a new string and send the XLIFF out to be translated. When the file comes back, check all the items with the state `needs-review-translation`. Change the state from `review` to `translated` or `final`, depending on your development process.

Although there are 11 predefined values, you usually need to use only 3 or 4 of them (new, `needs-review-translation`, `translated`, `final`). In the end-user application, these states typically appear as New, Review, Translated, and Final.

How you use the `state` attribute depends on your own workflow. If someone creates the XLIFF from the source code resources, the status is set to `new` for all new string values to be translated. It is then easier to see what needs to be done and to eliminate having to translate the same text more than once. When paying to have text translated, you typically pay by the word. You don't want to send over the same text to be translated over and over again.

The review status lets a subject domain expert review the translated text before approving it. The context of text is very important. A section of text translated from one language to another may be syntactically correct, but it might have the wrong meaning in the context of its use.

For example, the word *hood* in United States English and Great Britain English can refer to the part of a jacket that covers your head. In the context of a clothing application, *hood* is the same for both versions of English. If the app was is an automotive app, in United States English, the *hood* is the part of the car that covers the engine bay. In Great Britain English, that part of a car is referred to as a *bonnet*.

So you need to be very careful when using machine translation. On Google's translation page (`https://translate.google.com`), the default translation for *hood* is for the term that describes a head covering. When you use Google to translate *hood* from English to Spanish, the first match is for *capucha*, the clothing definition (see Figure 5-1).

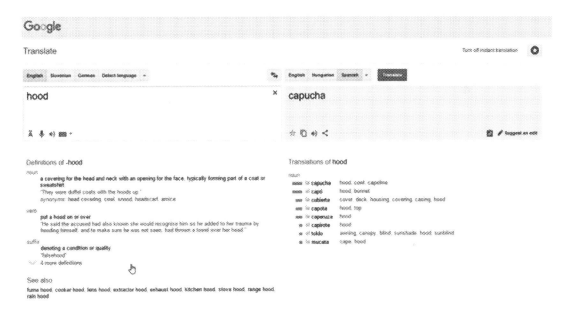

Figure 5-1. *Google Translate, English to Spanish*

As soon as you add some context by asking Google to translate the *hood of the car*, the translation becomes *el capó del coche*, using the automotive contextual version of hood.

***Figure 5-2.** Google Translate, English to Spanish*

If you are using XLIFF files, you need a way to edit the files and convert them to a format that your development tools can work with. These tools enable you to edit, import, and export the files.

The code examples in this book use the MAT from Microsoft, which generates XLIFF files from resource files. Table 5-3 shows some sample items defined in a resource file.

***Table 5-3.** Sample RESX Values*

Name	Value	Comment
AppDescription	Providing menus to the best of the restaurants	One-line description of the app
AppTitle	Island Menu	Title of the app as it should appear on the device
Welcome	Welcome	Simple salutation

The XLIFF file for the Spanish translation starts out looking like this:

```
<?xml version="1.0" encoding="utf-8"?>
<xliff version="1.2" xmlns="urn:oasis:names:tc:xliff:document:1.2" xmlns:xsi="http://www.
w3.org/2001/XMLSchema-instance" xsi:schemaLocation="urn:oasis:names:tc:xliff:document:1.2
xliff-core-1.2-transitional.xsd">
  <file datatype="xml" source-language="en" target-language="es" original="ISLANDMENUXF/
      RESOURCES/APPMAIN.RESX" tool-id="MultilingualAppToolkit" product-name="n/a" product-
      version="n/a" build-num="n/a">
    <header>
      <tool tool-id="MultilingualAppToolkit" tool-name="Multilingual App Toolkit" tool-
          version="4.0.1605.0" tool-company="Microsoft" />
    </header>
    <body>
      <group id="ISLANDMENUXF/RESOURCES/APPMAIN.RESX" datatype="resx">
        <trans-unit id="AppDescription" translate="yes" xml:space="preserve">
          <source>Providing menus to the best of the restaurants</source>
          <target state="new">Providing menus to the best of the restaurants</target>
          <note from="MultilingualBuild" annotates="source" priority="2">The one line
              description of the app</note>
        </trans-unit>
        <trans-unit id="AppTitle" translate="yes" xml:space="preserve">
          <source>Island Menu</source>
          <target state="new">Island Menu</target>
```

```
          <note from="MultilingualBuild" annotates="source" priority="2">The title of the
              app as it should appear on the device</note>
        </trans-unit>
        <trans-unit id="Welcome" translate="yes" xml:space="preserve">
          <source>Welcome</source>
          <target state="new">Welcome</target>
          <note from="MultilingualBuild" annotates="source" priority="2">A simple salutation</note>
        </trans-unit>
      </group>
    </body>
  </file>
</xliff>
```

After the English language text runs through the machine translation provided by MAT, the XLIFF
\<target\> elements are updated with the Spanish language equivalents, as shown here:

```
<?xml version="1.0" encoding="utf-8"?>
<xliff version="1.2" xmlns="urn:oasis:names:tc:xliff:document:1.2" xmlns:xsi="http://www.
w3.org/2001/XMLSchema-instance" xsi:schemaLocation="urn:oasis:names:tc:xliff:document:1.2
xliff-core-1.2-transitional.xsd">
  <file datatype="xml" source-language="en" target-language="es" original="ISLANDMENUXF/
    RESOURCES/APPMAIN.RESX" tool-id="MultilingualAppToolkit" product-name="n/a"
    product-version="n/a" build-num="n/a">
    <header>
      <tool tool-id="MultilingualAppToolkit" tool-name="Multilingual App Toolkit"
          tool-version="4.0.1605.0" tool-company="Microsoft" />
    </header>
    <body>
      <group id="ISLANDMENUXF/RESOURCES/APPMAIN.RESX" datatype="resx">
        <trans-unit id="AppDescription" translate="yes" xml:space="preserve">
          <source>Providing menus to the best of the restaurants</source>
          <target state="needs-review-translation" state-qualifier="mt-suggestion">Proporcionar
              menús al mejor de los restaurantes</target>
          <note from="MultilingualBuild" annotates="source" priority="2">The one line
              description of the app</note>
        </trans-unit>
        <trans-unit id="AppTitle" translate="yes" xml:space="preserve">
          <source>Island Menu</source>
          <target state="needs-review-translation" state-qualifier="mt-suggestion">Menú isla</target>
          <note from="MultilingualBuild" annotates="source" priority="2">The title of the
              app as it should appear on the device</note>
        </trans-unit>
        <trans-unit id="Welcome" translate="yes" xml:space="preserve">
          <source>Welcome</source>
          <target state="needs-review-translation" state-qualifier="tm-suggestion">Bienvenido</target>
          <note from="MultilingualBuild" annotates="source" priority="2">A simple salutation</note>
        </trans-unit>
      </group>
    </body>
  </file>
</xliff>
```

If you look at the AppTitle string resource, the untranslated XLIFF looked like this:

```
<trans-unit id="AppTitle" translate="yes" xml:space="preserve">
  <source>Island Menu</source>
  <target state="new">Island Menu</target>
  <note from="MultilingualBuild" annotates="source" priority="2">The title of the app as it
should appear on the device</note>
</trans-unit>
```

The source element is source language text, which in this example is Island Menu. The target element has the translated value. Because this text has not been translated, it has a default value of the original source value. It has the state attribute set to new, which signifies that it is a new text item to be translated. The note element brings in the comment from the resource file to provide context to the person doing the translation.

After the machine translation service completes, the target element for AppTitle now looks like this:

```
<target state="needs-review-translation" state-qualifier="mt-suggestion">Menú isla</target>
```

You can see three changes:

- The state has been changed to needs-review-translation, which is usually displayed as review.

- There is a new attribute, state-qualifier, which describes the state of a translated item, and there is a set of predefined values for state-qualifier (see Table 5-4).

- The value has been changed.

Table 5-4. *XLIFF 1.2 State-Qualifier*

Value	Description
exact-match	Indicates an exact match, which occurs when a source text of a segment is exactly the same as the source text of a segment that was translated previously.
fuzzy-match	Indicates a fuzzy match, which occurs when a source text of a segment is very similar to the source text of a segment that was translated previously (e.g., when the difference is casing, a few changed words, whitespace discrepancy, etc.).
id-match	Indicates a match based on matching IDs (in addition to matching text).
leveraged-glossary	Indicates a translation derived from a glossary.
leveraged-inherited	Indicates a translation derived from existing translation.
leveraged-mt	Indicates a translation derived from machine translation.
leveraged-repository	Indicates a translation derived from a translation repository.
leveraged-tm	Indicates a translation derived from a translation memory.
mt-suggestion	Indicates that the translation is suggested by machine translation.
rejected-grammar	Indicates that the item has been rejected because of incorrect grammar.
rejected-inaccurate	Indicates that the item has been rejected because it is incorrect.
rejected-length	Indicates that the item has been rejected because it is too long or too short.
rejected-spelling	Indicates that the item has been rejected because of incorrect spelling.
tm-suggestion	Indicates that the translation is suggested by translation memory.

The state-qualifier has been set to mt-suggestion, which signals that it was machine generated. When the text is translated by a professional language expert, the state-qualifier may be set to id-match, exact-match, or fuzzy-match.

When the XLIFF comes back from translation and is being reviewed, the translated item can be rejected. In that case, the state-qualifier is set to one of the rejected-* values. For example, in a medical form, there is a field labelled *Height*. The Spanish translation is *Estatura*. Another definition for height can be for elevation. In Spanish, *Altura* can be used for elevation. If the translation service had supplied *Altura* for *Height*, the reviewer would set the state-qualifier to rejected-inaccurate.

Another way to use the state-qualifier is to reject translations that are too long for the display. When writing mobile apps, space is a premium. If a translated value doesn't fit, the reviewer can set the state-qualifier to rejected-length. The comments of the source text should indicate that there is a space restriction.

The value of the target element contains the translated text. In this case, *Island Menu* came back as *Menú Isla*. It's a literal translation, but it may not make grammatical sense in Spanish. You can accept it, reject it, or change it. In this case, change it to *Menú de la Isla* with the MAT editor. Once it's been saved, the XLIFF for that item now looks like this:

```
<target state="translated">Menú de la Isla</target>
```

After final review, the reviewer sets the state as final, and the XLIFF looks like this:

```
<target state="translated">Menú de la Isla</target>
```

Index

© Christopher Miller 2017
C. Miller, *Cross-platform Localization for Native Mobile Apps with Xamarin*,
DOI 10.1007/978-1-4842-2466-3

Get the eBook for only $4.99!

Why limit yourself?

Now you can take the weightless companion with you wherever you go and access your content on your PC, phone, tablet, or reader.

Since you've purchased this print book, we are happy to offer you the eBook for just $4.99.

Convenient and fully searchable, the PDF version enables you to easily find and copy code—or perform examples by quickly toggling between instructions and applications.

To learn more, go to http://www.apress.com/us/shop/companion or contact support@apress.com.

Printed in the United States
By Bookmasters